PUBLIC SPEAKING

Effective Public Speaking Tips to Become Better Leader and Orator and Speak With Confidence

(A Step by Step Guide Helping You Find Your Voice and Skyrocket Your Public Speaking Career)

Scott Port

Published by Rob Miles

© **Scott Port**

All Rights Reserved

Conversation: Effective Public Speaking Tips to Become Better Leader and Orator and Speak With Confidence (A Step by Step Guide Helping You Find Your Voice and Skyrocket Your Public Speaking Career)

ISBN 978-1-989990-01-8

All rights reserved. No part of this guide may be reproduced in any form without permission in writing from the publisher except in the case of brief quotations embodied in critical articles or reviews.

Legal & Disclaimer

The information contained in this book is not designed to replace or take the place of any form of medicine or professional medical advice. The information in this book has been provided for educational and entertainment purposes only.

The information contained in this book has been compiled from sources deemed reliable, and it is accurate to the best of the Author's knowledge; however, the Author cannot guarantee its accuracy and validity and cannot be held liable for any errors or omissions. Changes are periodically made to this book. You must consult your doctor or get professional medical advice before using any of the suggested remedies, techniques, or information in this book.

Upon using the information contained in this book, you agree to hold harmless the Author from and against any damages, costs, and expenses, including any legal fees potentially resulting from the application of any of the information provided by this guide. This disclaimer applies to any damages or injury caused by the use and application, whether directly or indirectly, of any advice or information presented, whether for breach of contract, tort, negligence, personal injury, criminal intent, or under any other cause of action.

You agree to accept all risks of using the information presented inside this book. You need to consult a professional medical practitioner in order to ensure you are both able and healthy enough to participate in this program.

Table of Contents

INTRODUCTION 1

CHAPTER 1: YOU AS THE SPEAKER 3

CHAPTER 2: PREPARATION IS THE SOLUTION 11

CHAPTER 3: A SIMPLE STRUCTURE TO REMEMBER YOUR SPEECH 20

CHAPTER 4: TOP TEN MISTAKES TO AVOID 36

CHAPTER 5: DON'T FORGET SILENCE 41

CHAPTER 6: 15 TIPS TO BE BETTER AT PUBLIC SPEAKING . 45

CHAPTER 7: PUBLIC SPEAKING FEAR: IT'S A REAL THING . 57

CHAPTER 8: APPROACHING YOUR JOB INTERVIEWAS THOUGH YOU OWN THEM! 68

CHAPTER 9: SPEECH ORGANIZATION OPTIONS 72

CHAPTER 10: THE PACKAGING OF YOUR SPEECH 75

CHAPTER 11: TALKING WITH ANY ONE 94

CHAPTER 12: HOW TO USE THE PRINCIPLES OF PERSUASION 100

CHAPTER 13: PSYCHE UP 106

CHAPTER 14: GESTURES 109

CHAPTER 15: PUTTING IT ALL TOGETHER 123

CHAPTER 16: FIND COMMON GROUND AND FIND IT FAST. 126

CHAPTER 17: HEART LINK: THE VOICE AS AN INSTRUMENT 132

CHAPTER 18: IDENTIFY GOOD PUBLIC SPEAKERS AND STUDY HOW THEY DELIVER 152

CHAPTER 19: SPEAK FROM THE HEART 158

CHAPTER 20: THE VERY BEST WAY TO GET YOUR POINTS ACROSS 164

CHAPTER 21: PREPARING YOUR TV/RADIO INTERVIEW 169

CHAPTER 22: ELEVATING DAILY CONVERSATION 177

CHAPTER 23: HOW TO PREPARE TO GIVE THE SPEECH OF YOUR LIFE 181

CONCLUSION 194

Introduction

Today is the day that you start your quest, the day you start the journey from mere ordinary human to superhuman. What's that? You are afraid that you will never acquire all of the powers necessary to be a superhuman? Why, some of the best superheroes made do with only one or two specialized powers, and you, dear human are about to learn about one of the most rewarding of them all. The super power you are about to absorb is the ability to run a marathon.

Think that the average person can handle running just over 26 miles at one time? Of course not! That is why this is a superpower reserved for only those able to overcome the obstacles that are going to be thrown at them!

You will notice that this book does not include a specific training plan, or chart for how many miles you should be running.

That is because there are many, many runners on the path to becoming superhuman, and they have all started in a different place. If you are a brand new runner you will need a different chart than someone who has been running 5 and 10 ks, and are ready to move on up to the more serious races. Those charts exist, and are easy enough to find with the help of your favorite search engine. What you are going to find in this book are the basics of the whole deal.

It will be tough, physically and mentally. There will be days where the villainous duo Apathy and Self-Doubt will plague your every aching step over every grueling mile.

You will learn to vanquish those two jerks and whatever other minor villains that will pop up along the way. You are on your way to unleashing a new superpower. Now, where do most superhero stories begin?

Chapter 1: You As The Speaker

Attitude

The first thing that you should keep in mind is the fact that public speaking is not an artistic performance. Most people who achieve a great deal of success in public speaking reject the idea of winning the admiration of the audience. Preachers do not wish to be admired for their eloquence; they want to influence people's behavior and beliefs.

Just as teachers would not try to win the admiration of their students, they are more concerned in reshaping their student's attitudes and deliver new understanding. Your goal as the speaker is not gain the crowd's admiration for your poise or intelligence; your goal is to gain their agreement and respect to what you say.

Mastery of public speaking should not be a goal in itself, but it should serve as a means to attain noble and greater goals.

Stage Fright

Performance anxiety is a common challenge among speakers. Even successful and recognized public speakers face the same dilemma the moment they step on the platform.

This is a normal situation because being a speaker does not only mean showcasing your skills but the audience will also judge your personality, the quality of your logic and your worth as a person. They will form impressions involving every part of your character and this makes public speaking a frightening endeavor.

However, too much fear will lead to a boring, ineffective speech and dissatisfied listeners. The thing is, you are more concerned about what your performance on the stage will be like, afraid that you will sound ridiculous and worst make fool of yourself in front of a crowd.

Like in any other challenge, success in public speaking is gained through courage.

Almost every professional speaker will tell you that they gain this courage through a careful preparation.

Thorough preparation will give you the confidence that the topic you are about to present is beneficial to the audience and will help them to arrive at the right conclusion, make wiser decisions and survive challenging situations.

Planning and Preparation

Inexperienced speakers often waste their time in over thinking and experiencing entertaining anxiety about what will happen on the stage once they deliver the first paragraph. Thus, their effectiveness as a speaker is diminished because of needless concerns like whether they will look awkward, or forget some of the lines. Do not waste your time on worries. The stage of preparation will determine the success or failure of your presentation. Gather as many resources as you can.

Solicit reliable ideas from authorities on the topic and do thorough research for this will give you confidence in delivering your speech.

You can talk about a personal experience that are related to the topic as you will be more comfortable discussing your story. Don't try to memorize every line; you may not sound natural if you do. Know and understand the discussion. Recite your speech aloud and make some revisions if needed.

Fillers are not bad but repetition of filler words distracts the attention of your audience. Some will even find it annoying and they will be unsure of what it is that you are saying. They will doubt your ability and credibility. Practice will help you lessen the risk of stuttering and overusing of fillers.

Imagine that you are on the actual stage and practice with a timer so you'll know if your speech is lengthy or too short for the time allotted. Having someone to listen to your rehearsal is helpful so that you may solicit feedback from other person's perspective.

Develop the Right Thinking

Our minds work in four different ways- scientific, logical, expressionistic and rhetorical. The scientific mode presents facts precisely as they are and is devoid of personal feelings. Logical thinking is focused on the objective side of things and follows the dictate of logic. Expressionistic mode is also called egocentric because it presents things based solely on how you see it.

This type of thinking is prevalent among speakers who have few experiences. It depicts events and issues in a highly subjective manner, carrying the speaker's own beliefs and prejudices. However, public speaking requires the fourth mode of thinking which is called rhetorical.

It presents facts in their intrinsic state and its relationship to your own purposes, the meaning and its importance to the audience and its connection to the occasion. Surely, it will not be a good idea to give a speech about the need to implement death penalty if the listeners are members of a religious ministry.

You need careful attention to what the audience would feel once you present your point and bear in mind the nature of the occasion. Keep in mind that the event is for the benefit of the audience and not simply for you to voice out your subjective, biased view on a critical subject matter.

Your Message

Your message should carry substantial content and an excellent organization of the details. To do this, you must talk about the things that you already know or talk about a subject in which you have a genuine interest. But this does not mean that there is no need for you to visit the library to get some facts from valid resources.

The things that you should talk about are your own experiences, your own perception and your own knowledge - supported by all the information that you have gathered from authorities on the subject and through reasonable research.

Secondly, discuss a topic that is appropriate to the interests and needs of your audience. Pay attention to their age, social and economic status. Organizing your speech is probably easier to do because of the standard criteria that it should consist of an introduction, body and conclusion. All parts should effectively perform their specific functions.

The introduction or beginning of your speech should build an effective relationship with the listeners. It should not begin with the speaker's personal view or facts about the subject. It should be centered on the audience for the purpose of meeting where they are. The body or the discussion should carry points that will convince the audience that your message is worth listening to.

The goal of delivering this part is to make the audience understand your message and agree or respect your point of view.

The conclusion must lead toward what you want the listeners to do or think about the subject that you have presented. Know your purpose. Before drafting your speech, it is essential to make a careful note on your purpose of giving the speech in the first place. Is it to amuse, inform, inspire or persuade?

The purpose should be precise and should always have a connection to the audience and the subject matter. Have a vision of what you want to happen. This will be your basis and your guide in writing your drafts.

As mentioned earlier, you should not view public speaking as an artistic performance so reject your objective of being admired. Remember, good intentions always bring good results

Chapter 2: Preparation Is The Solution

You are a bone and anxiety is the dog that will chase you to hell. You can't completely get rid of it for it may strike just around the corner. If you kill it, another dog will just come hounding you. You can't totally eradicate anxiety. All you can hope for, in spite of feeling nervous and anxious, is to deliver your presentation with an ease and style that will make you come across as someone who's confident and knows what he's talking about. Aiming to be completely fearless is extremely difficult because butterflies will always find residence in your stomach whenever you speak in public. Even the most experienced and excellent of speakers still have to deal with anxiety every time they near a podium. It's what you do while the spotlight is on you that matters.

Habituation goes a long way in dealing with your communication apprehension. This psychological concept doesn't just apply to public speaking jitters but also to other fears as well. When you fear something, the ordinary response is to avoid the stimulus and get away from that negative emotion. However, in that case, you will never learn to build a resistance against your fear. If you face them and continually expose yourself to what you fear, it becomes familiar. In the case of presenting in front of people, the first time will almost always be nerve-wracking especially if you don't know your audience. There's something so scary about first times because you don't know what to expect and you are taken out of your comfort zone. However, when you make a habit of speaking in front of people, the repetition will make you more comfortable with the feat.

Repetition, however, is not enough. You also have to experience positive moments that you can draw inspiration from for future endeavors. Imagine speaking 2,000 times and getting embarrassed one way or another during those 2,000 times. Yes, you are the master of repetition but I will bet you anything you won't be able to bear speaking at the 2001th occasion. No matter how many times you do something, if nothing fruitful and positive comes from the experience, the likelihood of attempting it again will diminish because you don't have any reinforcement. This is why it's very important to take a lead role in creating the positive experiences that you want out of your public speaking engagements. And how do you do that? Well, you prepare, of course!

Work hard on your content

The first step toward success would be to create an excellent presentation or write a brilliant speech. No matter how well you present yourself in front of your audience, it won't matter if your content is low quality. In order to make your speech relevant and memorable to your listeners, take into consideration three important elements: audience, purpose, and manner.

Let's tackle the issue of your audience first. You have done a great job researching your topic and crafting a well-written speech. It's perfect. An English teacher would cry at your genius. But, if you made it for the wrong audience, then go home. Creating a presentation selling a multi-million apartment to an audience mostly composed of unprivileged individuals would be disastrous. The point is, you should first know and understand who you are talking to in order to be able to reach them with your message. This step is also vital to avoid conflict and minimize the chances of offending someone. Find out about their gender, occupation, age, backgrounds, and interests among other things to be able to figure out the right angle to approach with which to your audience.

Next, bear in the mind the purpose for doing this presentation in the first place and don't stray from your objective. It's not just about spouting all those words at all those people, you know. You are speaking because you want to motivate, encourage, persuade, inform, manipulate, ridicule, mock, entertain, patronize, and indulge. If you know your purpose for speaking, things will soon fall into place. You will then be able to point out what type of speech you'll be using, the right tone that you must set, the pace that you must take, so on and so forth.

Allot ample time to the creation stage

Don't slack off in making your presentation or writing your speech. Be serious in blocking off time for research, presentation development, outlining your speech, practicing it, etc. Don't cram because you will suffer the consequences in the end. To deliver a speech with ease requires effort and preparation.

You can prepare an outline for your speech or you can just settle for making note cards containing keywords, main points, and sub-points. Whatever you decide, remember the three main parts of a speech: the introduction, body, and conclusion.

The introduction is where you present the core of your message, where you will entice your listeners into paying ample attention to the rest of your content. It's very important because this is the part that should build anticipation for your audience and tell them what's in it for them if they care enough to give an ear on your speech. This is also where you can build your attention grabber.

Don't begin your speech with "Hello, I'm thankful to be here" or any other kind of generic greeting. Grab the attention of your audience by saying something powerful or interesting. Ask them a question or start with a quote relevant to your topic. You can also try citing an anecdote or a joke, a historic or current event, and a startling fact.

The body of the speech contains the details and elaborations on the points that you want to be conveyed to your listeners.

This is mainly where you strive to achieve your purpose. If you are motivating people into buying green products, incorporate the main reasons why they should and what would happen if they do otherwise in the body of your speech.

The conclusion will recapitulate the points that you have presented and will reiterate the main idea of your speech. Like the introduction, it should come off strong and memorable.

Watch what you eat

Avoid caffeinated drinks before speaking because they might make your hands shake. Avoid food that you know could upset your stomach because you don't want vomit to come out of your mouth mid-speech instead of words.

Hydrate yourself

Before going onstage, drink the necessary amount of water for the sake of your throat. It would be uncomfortable both for you and your listeners if you have a dry throat that requires you to keep coughing.

Practice

There is no substitute for rehearsal. Practice your speech before you deliver it to an audience. But uh-uh, don't just practice it in your head because it won't count. Unless the presentation that you have to do in front of people is also mental, you need to speak out loud.

Choose someplace private where you won't be interrupted and imagine that you really are in front of an audience. Mind your posture, your gestures, and where you are standing relative to your imaginary audience. Deliver your speech as many times as necessary before you feel comfortable delivering it.

It would also be advisable to ask for a friend to watch you talk while you practice. This way, you could rehearse initiating eye contact with him and can ask for feedback about the points you have to improve.

Also remember to time your speech if you don't have anyone with you to remind you of the time.

Rest well

Sleep well before the day of your event. You are no good with your eyes drooping with exhaustion just because you stayed up late for whatever reasons. Don't cram your presentation and be sure to leave ample time for resting.

Chapter 3: A Simple Structure To Remember Your Speech

If you are unhappy with your forgetfulness, know that you can deal with it effectively. Learning to remember is easy; the main thing is regular training.

Read aloud - this is how information is perceived by two senses, not only visually, but also by ear. In any case, the nerves that lead from the eyes to the brain are 20 times thicker than those that lead from the ear to the brain, so always try to get a visual impression. So, write down what you want to remember. Do not rush and do not try to remember something at the very last moment; devote more time to it.

In order to remember a fact, you should concentrate as much as possible, understand and comprehend it, and choose suitable images and pictures. If you constantly repeat and use the information you want to remember, it will be firmly deposited in your memory. For example, you can discuss the important points in your conversation with friends and family.

Additionally, connect existing knowledge with new ones in your mind, form many associations with the information you are trying to remember.

The following exercises are offered at public speaking courses:

Name from memory the names of all the writers, or poets, whom you can recall. If you recall 12-15 authors - a good result. You can also recall concepts from any field.

Very quickly, say out loud the objects that surround you. This will help to develop a quick reaction to what is happening. You will become less distracted.

Try performing the usual actions with your left hand (to develop the right hemisphere) if you are right-handed and vice versa.

Use Schulte tables to train visual memory (look for consecutive numbers in the table).

For several minutes, look at the landscape, person, subject, then close your eyes and try to recreate the image. You can try to draw it.

Use the "Roman Room" method - place memorized objects in your mind in a well-known room in a certain order.

Before we move on to a new topic, read these two texts that tell about the same event, the action "Help the child, and you will save the world."

Text 1

"Fundraising within the framework of the charity media marathon "Help the child and you will save the world" will begin this week. According to the regional branch of the London's Children's Fund, the official start of the marathon will be given on June 1. Within three months, there will be meetings between children and writers, performances by children's creative groups, sports relay races, charity shows of children's performances, and other events. Among the goals and projects of the fund, the main ones are three that are planned to be developed at the marathon: "Outback Children," "Children's Health," and "Believe in You."

The project "Outback Children" is a long-term project; it operates only in the Chelmsford Region. After the marathon, within the framework of this project, orphans will have the opportunity of labor rehabilitation: in some orphanages, they will build an apiary, deliver agricultural machinery and animals. As part of the Children's Health project, it is planned to improve the conditions for the treatment of children in the Regional Children's

Tuberculosis Hospital. During the marathon, donations to fund projects will be accepted.

This week it will be possible to make a charity call to 770-770 (the cost of the call is 20 dollars). In the near future, mobile operators in the region will determine a single number for SMS donations. Mini-marathons will be held in many regions of the area, and donations will also be accepted there from June 1. Funds collected in the territories will be accumulated in the general account for monitoring, and then returned to the regions. Donations will be accepted until September 20.

In October, a reception will be held with the governor of the region, where the most active participants in the marathon will be marked."

Text 2

"We all know that there are no other people's children ... But there are abandoned ones. Even in such a small, young, and bright city like ours, there are orphans. They have no mom and no dad. There is no one to intercede for them, and they themselves cannot intercede for themselves, they are small.

And this is not right, because these children are not to blame for the fact that they were not lucky to be born in a family where they would be surrounded by care and love.

There are more of us, adults and caring people, we are able to help these children and brighten up their lives. The goal of our small initiative group is to draw the attention of network users to the problems of orphans who find themselves without guardianship. We have the strength and desire to be useful to them.

We all come from childhood. It is wrong to divide children into "friends" and "strangers." Any of your help that you can provide to children - whether it is to hand over clothes or just bring a pair of diapers to the aid collection point is important and valuable. After all, these children have no one, and the stones will not help us. If you are compassionate for someone else's misfortune and you have every opportunity to help orphans, we will be glad to cooperate!

At the moment, our action is at the start stage, and a lot needs to be done in such a short time! The first thing I will turn to you for is that I need people who can draw posters on Whatman sheets. Draw bright, interesting, and with a soul. We also need help with the issue of large boxes or large bags for collecting things. And, most importantly, volunteers who are ready to spend several hours at collection points.

A list of necessary things exists, but I would like to emphasize once again that any help would be appropriate. The clothes are in good condition, not worn shoes, furniture, felt-tip pens, drawing albums, books.

We plan to start collecting things from Monday. I beg you, do not remain indifferent."

What feelings does each text evoke? What are the emotions? Do they encourage action, do you want to participate in the action and help children? Why does text No. 2 make a greater impression, is remembered, and after reading it, there is a desire to help the initiative group at least with something? Thanks to what the author of the second text created an emotional mood? Think about it in your free time, but for now, let's move on to theory.

The most important quality of the speaker and his speech is the ability to capture the feelings and consciousness of people to influence their imagination. Therefore, in speech, both rational and emotional aspects should be equally present. Emotionality is a necessary and important quality of speech, and it is called imagery. It is she, acting on the feelings, brings a person to the act. An emotional speech occurs when the speaker knows how to feel strongly and has a vivid imagination that helps him create images of what he is talking about. The speaker's task is to see what is happening, feel it, and be able to convey it, but words alone are not enough. The image is important. You need to vividly represent what you are talking about.

This is what distinguishes the two above texts. When you read the second text, the imagination vividly draws orphans who need help and protection, clothes, diapers, collection points, posters on sheets of Whatman paper. The author is very concerned about the topic of orphans, the condition of the children is felt, drawn through their own souls. The author understands what he is talking about; he sees it! And conveys in words. And when you read the text, you also see this - the clothes are in good condition, not worn shoes, furniture, felt-tip pens, drawing albums, books - that's all.

Note that when we talk about the figurativeness of speech, we have in mind the original essence - the speaker's ability to think in images. And only in second place after this is the ability to convey the image through the means of lexical expression. If the speaker manages to develop these two skills and combine them, he will be able to occupy the highest level of honor in society. It is then that we can say that this speaker has eloquence. And to develop these skills, it takes years of daily work to compose and deliver speeches.

Ever wondered why the tales heard in childhood, people remember until old age? The thing is that fairy tales are written in figurative language, and it makes a person have the strongest impressions!

A person can learn to think in images! To do this, you need to develop an artistic perception of the world - to see the image. And to search for words in order to most accurately display it, it is at the moments of the search for words that image is more clearly drawn, and then a person can convey it.

For example, looking at the clouds, describe them with words - shredded, fluffy, milky white, like thick sour cream, lead black. Watching a cat, look for exact words to describe its appearance and habits. Outline your beloved dog so precisely and figuratively that a friend can easily distinguish it from a dozen of them like her.

For example, try to describe a person's eyes. The simple word "eyes" will not convey their image to us because they are different. Hazel, saucer eyes, blue, crafty, funny, sparkling, vibrant, alert, velvet, black, Asian, slanting, narrow, large, icy, bottomless, round, transparent, squinted, colorless, fast, shiny, cloudy, open, radiant, pensive, mischievous, wagging, truthful, bluish-gray, embarrassed, happy, angry, cold, surprised, reproached, clear, furious, attentive, kind...

Develop a habit of observing the world and discover that it is all alive. Even at home. And iron buses, and candy wrappers on the sidewalk. See their images. For example, a bus may be just off the factory assembly line, young, cheerful, full of strength, energy, the desire to move and smile at traffic lights. Or it may be old, having exhausted its resource, and therefore tired, with its sides swollen with time, squatting and frowning.

Give birth to images. Remember the anecdotal cases from life and be able to figuratively talk about them. Look for an emotional approach to the listener.

Learning how to create and transmit images will help.

Exercises

1. Portrait of a Friend

Create a verbal portrait of your friend so that a stranger can recognize him from hundreds of passengers at the station. Having made the description, let it read to someone who is familiar with the prototype of the portrait and ask him to guess who is reflected in the description. If it turned out weakly, continue to paint a portrait, looking for more and more accurate words, describing more and more vivid, imaginative details. Until the "portrait" is easily recognized even by outsiders.

2. Figurative Words

When there is a minute of free time, look for an item to describe. For example, when you see a crow sitting on a tree, think up words and images that fully reflect its habits and character. Compare it with the character and habits of man, with natural phenomena. Look for words to reflect her accurate portrait.

In the subway, observe people. Among the mass of passengers on the excavator platform and in the car, see the Person, the Personality of a person that distinguishes him from others. And describe it in words.

Set yourself an ordinary teacup, compare it with a person, elements of nature, animals, and find figurative words to describe this long-familiar everyday object.

The ability to think and speak figuratively depends on how much a person can use the energy of the hemisphere of the brain responsible for creativity. There are ways in which this hemisphere can be developed.

3. Left-Handed

Learn to write and draw with your left hand. It will not be easy, but only at first. Over time, the written will be read without difficulty. Engage your left hand in any situation. Learn to keep a spoon, a glass in it. Play badminton with the racket in your right or left hand. Perform a ton of other small actions with your left hand. For example, thread a needle. Try to knit not from the right - to the left, but rather from the left - to the right. Band up your right hand and type on the computer with your left hand. Overcome the feeling of helplessness and the desire to return to the usual mode of action. And as the left-hand gains strength and begins to cope with operations unusual for it, the creative hemisphere will come to life. Bright, creative ideas will appear, imaginative thinking will be easier to develop, speech will change, and it will go easily and smoothly,

Note: If the person is left-handed, then we develop the right hand.

4. Juggler

Take two small balls and juggle. Having thrown the ball from the left hand to the right, watch its flight. When it is about halfway through the distance, throw the second ball from the right hand into the left. While it overcomes half the distance, manage to catch the first ball with his right hand while watching the ball falling into his left hand. And so throw and catch balls continuously.

This helps visual imagination.

5. Image of the Word

In the phrase below, disassemble the logic of each word, following it with your eyes and taking your time: "trading in seeds, cucumbers, and pies." See the image mentally, save it, and, holding in front of you, pronounce the phrase out loud.

Using the same method, work with the following words and phrases: "military", "technical team at the office", "mother shaking a child", "teacher", "student", "pioneer", "theater director", "director", "Cashier at the station", "history of the state".

Having mastered the method, use it when preparing a public speech. This will give your speech a great expression.

Chapter 4: Top Ten Mistakes To Avoid

I'm not telling you this to frighten you, but to educate you so you can have a much more professional presence on stage. These top ten mistakes should be considered as you are writing the speech and as you are practicing the speech. Be sure you're not doing any of these or you will lose your audience.

#1 Lazy Profanity

Profanity can be used in some speeches, and in some cases it's entertaining. If your audience is just some friends at a small, close wedding, profanity can be okay. If it's a business meeting, strangers, an educational speech, or anything professional in just the slightest, profanity is not okay. It's also not okay to use excessive profanity because people will begin to wonder if you don't know how to articulate using anything else. So keep profanity to a minimum when it comes to being with friends, and keep it out entirely when you're not in close company.

#2 Lateness

If you're late, you're insulting the audience. Even if it's a good excuse, you've still wasted their time. So do everything in your power to be at the venue where you will speak **early** so you don't have the opportunity to be late.

#3 Leering

It's awkward, but it's true. Men **and** women both leer at people they're attracted to, but when you're giving a professional speech, keep your eyes on nothing but other eyes. No up and down looks, especially onstage.

#4 Pollyannaish

The word translates to being overoptimistic. Take, for example, someone who has just experienced a natural disaster and nothing is okay at the moment, but they keep going and claim everything is okay right then. It kind of undermines their professionalism.

#5 Being Flighty

When it comes to doing a speech, let's say you promise to deliver an answer to a question in the introduction, and when you get the conclusion, the audience is wondering where the answer was. That's being a little flighty. They don't know the point of your speech then.

#6 Being Disorganized

If your speech is disorganized and you're trying to get a point across, people are going to wonder if you're really a reliable source. They're also going to wonder what the point was of sitting there listening to you talk. So you should be organized in every aspect of your speech.

#7 Inarticulateness

Have you ever been in a conversation with someone who used like all the time when it wasn't necessary or they rambled about something without really getting to the point? That's being inarticulate, and it can be very annoying for an audience. Get to the point and never use filler words such as like in your speech. You might be professional and well educated, but being inarticulate will make you come across as someone who's never stepped inside a school or learned any type of grammar.

#8 Secrecy

Speeches are meant to convey a message or a point, not to make the audience wonder about your personal life or your professional life. Don't be secretive in a business speech or the employees are going to think you're hiding something, well, because you probably are. Keep the secrecy out of the speech.

#9 Overpromising

The heart of selling to an audience is promising the maximum you can but being consistent with what you can actually deliver. Therefore, never promise an audience something you can't give them that very second. Someone might call you on it and you'll look bad, really bad.

#10 Cheating and Lying

Just like in a relationship, cheating and lying to your audience is not going to go over well. They trust you to tell them the facts and the truth. If you don't, everything you just told them is going to go out the window. They won't take away **any** points from your speech if you lie to them.

Now you know the top ten mistakes made by other speech writers and public speakers, so let's take a look at the more personal side of the process, overcoming stage fright.

Chapter 5: Don't Forget Silence

Silence happens to be a very powerful tool that can be used when speaking to someone. Pausing can help you lay emphasis on your charismatic nature and not make you look like someone who cannot stop babbling. It gives people the time to understand what you are saying and absorb your ideas.

Here is how you can use speech to your advantage:

Pausing between Major Parts of Speech

Remember that your audience will only be able to process your speech when it comes in smaller or more manageable pieces. A disadvantage associated with public speaking is that people tend to present one major point after another without stopping, thereby overloading the audience. This means that the listener is receiving too much data without a proper break and a conclusion. The speech should be such that there should be a structure to it and a pause or silence in between each to divide it.

Silence Helps Your Audience Absorb More Information

When it comes to telling your listener something important that you want him or her to absorb and retain, you must use the power of silence to do so. If you happen to pause at the right time to help the listener process the information, the audience will respond to it in real time. Remember that they are not reading a book where they can simply re-read a paragraph to grasp it. A short stint of silence can help them grasp the main point and analyze it in their mind.

Use of Dramatic Pause

A dramatic pause is a tool used by stage actors during performances. This pause is taken at a time when the audience is expecting something important and binds together the entire conversation and, just when the crucial line or piece of information is delivered, the audience bursts into a thunderous clap. Similarly, you have to take a pause just when your listener gets very excited to hear what you have to say, which can impact the whole speech. Remember that the length of the pause will always seem longer to you than your listener so you have to drag it just enough for the listener to feel like the gap was just right.

Ask a Question and then Go Quiet

When you wish to engage the listener, you have to ask them many questions. In fact, you have to ask them relevant questions that you want answers to. Apart from them, you must also ask questions to which they will not have an answer to and go quiet. This will make them think and will grab their attention. You have to pause until such time as they come up with an answer.

Using Silence to Control the Pace

When you speak to someone, it is important to make sure that you go about it at the right speed. If you are too fast, the listener will not understand you and, if you are too slow, the listener will get bored so it is important to make use of pauses to ensure that you control the pace at which you speak. If you pause for no reason, the listener will think you are nervous so it is best to know when to take a pause to make the speech more impactful.

Chapter 6: 15 Tips To Be Better At Public Speaking

Now that you know how to gain complete control of performance anxiety, you can start speaking in public. However, overcoming stage fright doesn't necessarily make you a good public speaker.

Overcoming stage fright is simply the first basic step to becoming a better public speaker. If you want to improve your public communication skills and take it to the next level, you must enhance your public speaking abilities.

The 15 amazing public speaking tips below can help you do that:

1: Practice Your Speech

Practice definitely makes perfect; this is exactly what will happen to your public speaking abilities when you repeatedly rehearse your speech. The more you practice something, the more command you get on it and the easier it comes to you. Rehearse what you have to speak a hundred times and see how beautifully you will be able to speak.

2: Own The Place

Have you watched Bill Clinton give a public speech? If yes, you would have noticed that whenever Clinton addresses his audience, he makes the crowd feel that he owned that place. This is exactly what you need to do because when you feel you own the entire place, you become sure of yourself and relax. Feel that you have conquered the world and everyone is impressed by you. This makes you feel confident, which helps deliver a powerful speech. Here is what you need to do to own the place.

How to Own the Place

Know the place well: To feel as if you actually own a place, it is important to properly work that place and know it in detail. Arrive at the venue a couple of hours before addressing your audience, or visit it a day before the big day and study it.

Find out how big or small the stage is, and plan how to use it efficiently. Check out if your voice echoes in that room or not, or what type of mic setting will work best in that venue. This information will help you plan your public speaking accordingly, which will help you feel comfortable in that place and speak like a boss.

Dress sharply: The second tactic is to dress sharp. When you are smartly dressed, you feel good about yourself. This gives you the confidence to feel like you actually own the place.

Dressing sharply means dressing smartly in accordance with the occasion. If the event is a formal one, get your suit or tuxedo ready, a pantsuit in case of females; but if it's casual or semi-formal, then a crisp, collared shirt with neatly tailored pants will work well too.

3: Work On Your Body Language

Public speaking isn't merely about speech fluency. A good public speaker isn't one who can speak a thousand words clearly and smoothly. Instead, an impressive public speaker is someone who can empower the audience and make them feel involved in the speech. This is only possible when you have the right body language.

The right body language is one that exudes confidence and courage. Walk in the room in a manner that loudly speaks of your brilliant skills. For that, you need to correct your body posture. Stand straight, ensuring that your spine isn't slouched or hunched back. Your head needs to be straight, chin up, shoulders straight and firm and chest open. Next, whenever you speak publicly, keep your arms open and your legs at least knee width apart. In addition, if you intend to use gestures, make them firmly and not trembling: a shaky body is a show of a lack of confidence.

4: Maintain Direct Eye Contact With Your Audience

Oprah Winfrey is one of the most brilliantly interesting and inspiring public speakers. If you have observed her style closely, you would have noticed that she maintains direct eye contact with her guests and audience.

When she is addressing the audience, people actually feel that she is talking to them. This is one reason her audience becomes deeply engrossed in her speech. This one small thing, eye contact, distinguishes a professional and seasoned public speaker from an amateur.

To convince your audience, you need to establish direct eye contact with them. Just look at them softly in the eye and keep talking, and within seconds, they will become involved in your speech.

To practice maintaining good eye contact, first, try speaking in front of a mirror, then a supportive person. Practice establishing proper eye contact with them. Constant practice will definitely help you get there.

5: Never Read Your Speech

When addressing an audience, never read your entire speech from the paper. Yes, do keep small notes, so you can remember important points on time, but reading directly from the paper is a big NO. Reading from paper during the entire speech disassociates your audience and makes them feel that you don't care much about them, which is why you didn't take time to memorize your speech.

6: Tailor Your Speech To Your Audience

Knowing your audience is imperative to being a good public speaker. Before drafting a speech, know what your audience wants, what they aim to learn from your speech, and their preferences.

For that, you have to extensively research your audience. This knowledge will help you create content that actually inspires and motivates your audience, making them want to listen to you repeatedly.

7: Be Loud, Clear, And Polite

It is important for a public speaker to speak loudly and clearly so that everyone can hear. Make sure to speak in a loud, firm, and clear voice and utter each word in an understandable manner. When you speak loudly, make sure your tone does not become rash. People do not appreciate garish speakers; speak in a polite, humble, and authoritative tone.

8: Raise And Lower Your Voice

Your voice pitch plays an important role in engaging others. If your pitch is increasingly high, your listeners will leave the venue in minutes. Similarly, if your pitch is extremely low, your audience will fall sleep.

Maintain a balanced pitch raised and lowered according to different instances in your speech. If you need to stress a point, make sure to raise your voice and speak words firmly. If you need to express your dismay on something, you must lower it and make your tone seem disappointed.

Adding expressions into your tone will add an interesting and engaging touch to your speech, attracting people towards what you are saying.

9: Use Facial Expressions

Your facial expressions need to align with the tone of your voice. This makes your speech more engaging. If you are talking about a serious issue, make sure your face is grim and serious to convey this. This simple tactic can increase your audience's interest in your speech by manifolds.

10: Pace Around

Standing firmly in one spot speaks loudly of a lack of self-confidence. Pace around when you speak because this gesture radiates confidence. It makes people feel that you know what you're doing and are sure of yourself. When people can feel your confidence, they know you are a professional and start taking interest in your speech.

11: Make Your Speech An Interactive Session

Often, audiences don't listen to what the speaker is saying; they're busy using their phones or yawning because your speech is boring. To convert your speech from boring to interesting, have an interactive session. Involve people in your speech by asking them questions, asking for their input, or giving them different activities. This gives them something interesting to do, making them listen to you.

12: Use Multimedia

Words are not always enough to engage people and draw them towards your speech. This is where multimedia comes in; pictures and images can breathe life into your verbose speech, making it exciting. You can create a PowerPoint presentation, show pictures, and videos relevant to your speech, and use placards.

13: Be Who You Are

While it is important to have a mentor who inspires you to become a good public speaker, you must not imitate your idol. That person already exists and people know them; why should an audience make an effort to listen to you if you're a copycat?

People are always craving for something fresh and different; which is why, you MUST be yourself while speaking in public. Do not shy away from exhibiting your unique identity. For that, embrace yourself and use affirmations to reaffirm your value.

14: Eat A Nutritious Meal Before Creating, And Presenting Your Speech

Your brain needs to be alert and active when you prepare your speech and when you present it. For that, you need to feed your body a healthy, nutritious meal regularly, especially when you have to write your speech and before speaking publicly.

Make sure to eat a meal loaded with protein because proteins contain tyrosine, an important amino acid that creates epinephrine and dopamine in the body. Dopamine and epinephrine regulate mental alertness. Therefore, before drafting your speech, and addressing your audience, eat meat, seafood, and eggs to ensure your body is firing on all pistons.

15: Have a Contingency Plan

What if your video presentation doesn't work, or there is a glitch in the multimedia? What would you do in that case? Most people start fretting in that situation. Since you plan to become an excellent public speaker, work like a pro and have a plan B ready for contingencies. Always have two to three plans so you can conveniently switch to the other plan when the first one doesn't work. This way, you won't waste your audience's time, something they would truly appreciate, and you'll be able to deliver your speech successfully.

With those amazing tips, you can become a good public speaker. However, in order to be a great public speaker, you need to be able to wow your audience. Let us look at this in the following chapter.

Chapter 7: Public Speaking Fear: It's A Real Thing

What causes public speaking fear? It's the mere fact of standing in front of a crowd – whether you know them or not – and talking.

You may have worked for weeks on a subject; learned the materials inside and out and prepared the presentation. The anxiety was there, but you ignored it. When it's time to talk to your audience, you suddenly feel weak in the knees, your brain goes blank, and you stutter.

Public speaking fear – it's really a thing!

This fear is real, and it's a phobia. Recent studies show that approximately 40 percent of people are afraid to speak publicly. And, everybody has some fear of public speaking – be it minor or major.

It doesn't really matter if you're talking to a minute number of people or a lot of people, the fear of public speaking can affect you in some way.

In fact, even the most experienced public speakers have become nervous before giving an important speech.

The anxiety can impact you in various ways such as the inability to speak at all or not giving it your best.

Whatever the impact it has, the signs of the fear are clear:

Rapid heartbeat

Sweaty, shaky hands

Dizziness

Nausea

Blank mind

Shortness of breath

Public speaking fear happens for an array of reasons, but the fear can actually be divided into two distinct categories:

Experienced-based

Historically-based

A Look At Historically-Based Public Speaking Fear

In the past, humans lived in tribes, which instilled fears that helped them to survive. A tribe usually consisted of 30 to 100 members with a single male leader.

The leader was the person who ensured the tribe's survival. Now, consider if another person tried to make a speech in front of the rest of the tribe – someone who isn't the leader.

The tribe's leader may take that as being trying to overthrow them. In most cases, the penalty for this was death.

The reality is that public speaking wasn't regarded as safe. For historical reasons, it's the key reason people are afraid of public speaking.

The Evolutional Psychology talks about situations such as these. The key to remember is that fear is irrational. There's no way to explain it for others to understand, but understanding how the world was tens of thousands of years ago may give some answer behind it.

A Look At Experience-Based Public Speaking Fears

Besides the psychological reasons behind public speaking fears, there are some reasons in your life that can explain the fear.

For example, your language is your conversation. When you talk, you often do it with another person. The body's neurological system is used to taking part in conversations.

It's not used to paying mind to the internal processes it goes through when talking. Why? It's an automatic response, which allows a person to focus on the conversation taking place.

When you take part in an unknown activity, you may feel intimidated by it. Why is that? You don't have the experience for it just yet. You're unable to use your voice properly or know how to look just right at a person.

You may not know the kind of language patterns you must have during the speech, and that there is another way of using language in a speech.

Past experiences also affect your fear. If you've had an embarrassing experience of talking in front of a group of people, the fear of it happening again is real. Experienced-based fear is a normal part of public speaking fear.

What Does This Mean?

Simply put, public speaking fear hinders you from being able to speak clearly and without hesitation at a public event. You may even find yourself unable to get in front of the audience because of that fear.

The first reason is based on who humans are with the second reason being based on what you've already experienced in life.

Rational vs. Irrational Fears

Before you can deal with the aspect of public speaking fear, you have to understand your view of the fear you have.

Rational Fears

These are fears that can be explained – something that could cause or lead to harm either emotionally or physically.

Some examples of this include:

Dangerous items – knives, guns, etc.

Dangerous situations – floods, earthquakes, volcanoes, etc.

Dangerous activities – skydiving, skiing, tightrope walking, etc.

The fears of some activities, situations and items are thought of as rational due to the danger they can impose on your life.

Fears can save you when you need it most. You can see fear as something positive, especially if it helps you to survive.

Irrational Fears

These are fears that prevent you from being the best you can be (not help you to live). For instance, if a dog bites you, you may have a fear of dogs for the rest of your life.

If you're scared in the dark by someone, you may never want to be alone in the dark again.

The fear mechanism isn't perfect, and work must be done to address the fears you do have.

You should always understand your rational fears – perhaps even encourage them. It's the irrational fears you need to be mindful of – the ones that you need to overcome and move past.

Public Speaking Fear: Rational Or Irrational?

Does public speaking cause you harm? In the past, public speaking could be dangerous, which is why it was rational to be afraid of speaking out.

Due to the rationale of this fear, people now see as being Evolutional Psychology. Does this same principle apply today though?

Hypothetically, it can. If you're talking to a large group of hostile individuals, you may have an emotional fear. If you're in a gang and need to talk to the other members, you could experience physical harm.

For the most part, though, public speaking is safe. There is no real reason to be afraid of your classmates or co-workers when presenting them with information or products.

The fear for public speaking today is considered irrational!

How Can You Overcome Irrational Fear?

If you are to overcome and move past your public speaking fear, you have to remember and understand that the fear is irrational.

There are two ways in which you do this:

Subconscious — You need to work on the processes that take place in the brain even when you don't know they are taking place. The idea is to eliminate the fear from your mind.

Methods — Certain methods can help you through public speaking events even if the fear is still there.

The more methods you use, the more experience you gain. The more experience you gain, the more confidence you feel in yourself. The more confident you are, the less fear will rule you.

Keep in mind that every speech — whether or not you've practiced less fear — will be fearful. The less you give into it, the better off you will.

Think of your mind has being a complex machine. It runs a plethora of programs at one time – some you are aware of; others you are not. Those you are not aware of are in your subconscious.

When talking publicly, you have two processes in your head:

The first one is positive and tells you to knock the dead with your speech.

The second one is negative and tells you that you can't do it.

You can eliminate the fear you have about public speaking, but you must use methods to do it. Since it's a subconscious process, you know it's dealing with your unconscious mind. What are some of these methods?

NLP (Neuro-linguistic programming

Hypnosis

Belief system

Learning techniques may help you to address your fears but will not eliminate them entirely. It's a positive aspect and can help you speak better in public.

However, it doesn't get rid of the fear even though it does make it easier to talk in public.

Should you use it when working on your subconscious mind? Absolutely! If you learn the techniques, you will never perfect your speeches, and each speech will still be an effort to get through.

Chapter 8: Approaching Your Job Interviewas Though You Own Them!

Summary

A lot pegs on a job interview. It could be a life-changing experience in many situations. It is no wonder that more than half the people are scared to death about facing interviews.

Approaching Your Interview as though You Own Them!

So you got that all-important call for the job interview that you were rooting for. Now, everything depends on how the interview goes. Enough to put pressure upon your shoulders, right? But do you think you are going to nail that interview if you go with all that pressure?

You must approach your job interviews with care. You have to show them that you know your stuff, but at the same time you must not come across as brash. You have to walk a fine line here — not seem insolent but at the same time you must not seem submissive either. The impression you generate during your job interview stays with you throughout your career life.

Here is how you must prepare yourself.

1. Tell yourself that you have got this interview. Let it seem real to you. Now, you have to become practical about it. You should not let this chance pass you by.

2. Repeat this several times — "They called me because they found something good in my résumé". This will help boost your confidence like nothing else can. You will realize that there's some quality about you that they liked.

3. The day you go for the interview, don't work yourself too much. Dress subtly, and do some breathing exercises before entering the interviewing hall. Yes, this helps.

4. Introduce yourself to them with a firm handshake if within reach. If not,

make good eye contact which shows them you aren't nervous.

5.   You must have already researched on what they ask during interviews.

Prepare your pitch well. The advantage here is that you don't have to break the ice, because they will speak with you first. They will ask you to walk them through your résumé. You should have this ready. Focus on the positive points and make sure that they hear them, but don't dwell on a particular area too much.

6.   If there is something quirky about your résumé, they will definitely ask you about that. Keep a reply ready. You must know that it is the most fruitful if you could be honest in your replies.

7.   Most times, they will ask you your opinion on something. This is the clinching point actually. Make sure you say something creative. Don't hold back, and don't cross any lines. Remember that this question might come out of the blue,

when you think everything has relaxed. Be prepared for such assaults.

8. They may also ask you your strengths and weaknesses. Again, be upfront and honest. Don't overemphasize your plus points. Don't dwell too much on your weaknesses. Act as though they are quite commonplace, everyone has them.

You have done your best. Now, wait for them to decide whether they can take you. If the call doesn't come, you can at least seek solace in the fact that you did not make a mistake.

Chapter 9: Speech Organization Options

In collecting and organizing information for your speech, consider the following style options:

☐ Temporal organization is when you arrange information based on when it happened or when it will happen. Chronology is important to avoid confusing your audience. While movies and books can get away with jumping from one time-frame to another, a listening audience has a harder time keeping up.

☐ Cause and effect explains how A causes B. A speech about how illegal immigration ruins an economy can be emotional, but unless you establish cause and effect, it's neither informative nor factual.

☐ Compare and contrast is an excellent way to highlight similarities and differences. It can also make a complex topic easier to understand. If you're trying to explain the Eurozone crisis to an American audience, for example, it would help to cite economic similarities in the American context to make your points clearer.

☐ Topical design arranges information according to specific categories. If you're doing a speech on the US government, for example, you can arrange your information according to federal and state, or into executive, legislative, and judicial branches.

☐ Spatial pattern organizes information according to how they physically relate to each other. Whether you're discussing parts of the body or world geography, arranging your information in such a way that people know where things are greatly increases their comprehension.

☐ Credibility is established by providing three things: **statistics**, **specific instances**, and **testimony**. Statistics requires raw numbers, such as percentages and averages. Specific instances give weight to your statements, while testimonies make it personal. If you are trying to inform or to convince, credibility is extremely vital, or you will lose your audience. In a speech simply meant to entertain, it is not necessary.

Chapter 10: The Packaging Of Your Speech

I'm quite certain that at least once in your life you have heard the saying that what matters is not entirely what you say but how you say it. That is fairly true. In some cases, the information you're providing might be just fine. However, the way you gesticulate or move can affect whether or not your audience decides to trust in your words. First impressions are essential to the way we interact with other people.

In the previous chapter, we spoke about the backend of your speech. In this chapter, we're more focused on how we present it. The appearance of your speech plays an equally important role as the content.

Language

The ways you speak to a good friend, your parents, and your boss are (hopefully) different. When publicly speaking, the language and voice you use should also be significantly different, depending on whom you're addressing (Carnegie, 1962). Audiences can differ in many ways. If you followed what we discussed in chapter 1, at this point, you should already have a profile of your audience.

Having such a profile in hand can lead you to make an assessment of the characteristics of your audience. Figure out if there is a hierarchical structure that you're expected to observe. For instance, your audience might be high-ranking officials within an organization; thus, you're expected to use respectful language. It can be, though, the other way around, and the audience might expect you to play an authority role. Or you might realize that the atmosphere is quite casual and there's no need to build so many barriers around you. Ask yourself who your audience is and what position you are fulfilling before them.

Likewise, think of how connected the audience is with the given topic. Have you ever been to the doctor who uses a language that's completely foreign to you? It's annoying, right? Well, don't do that yourself! An additional question for you to answer is the level of expertise of your audience. If a doctor has a presentation for a medical conference, they can certainly use very technical vocabulary, but the situation drastically changes if the audience is a more generic one.

An interesting trick is to ask yourself, "How would I explain this topic that I'm an expert at to my grandmother?" (This is assuming that your grandma isn't an expert in that topic too.) In other words, put it in the simplest terms possible. As we'll discuss in the next chapter, the key is to find the balance. Use your area of expertise as your ally so that you appear as a knowledgeable yet approachable speaker.

There's also a debate as to what choice of words and tone of voice to use. For starters, the best advice is to be yourself—not only to be yourself per se but to be the best version of yourself (Duarte, 2010). In chapter 1, we briefly mentioned that authenticity is one of the characteristics that make a speech great. Language is one of the ways by which an audience can realize whether you're an authentic speaker.

You may have in mind a particular speaker that you consider to be excellent. Spend some time watching that person's speeches and analyze their style. You'll soon find that the speaker has certain characteristics that are natural to them. Those characteristics are part of their persona and the key factor why people remember them. In the very same way, think of what your personal characteristics are when speaking. You can make those characteristics your signature. This will create consistency.

Making Your Speech Visual by Assessing Your Audience

There's a way in which you can make your speech "visual." This is especially useful because you should keep in mind that there are different ways in which people understand information. Hopefully, you'll encounter auditory learners. This type of people may be staring at something else and apparently aren't paying you attention. However, they have the skill of listening and digesting every single detail you're expressing. However, auditory learners are not the majority of people; thus, it's wise not to focus on them only (Welsh, 2011). The other two types are kinesthetic and visual learners.

As the name suggests, visual learners rely heavily on observing to understand concepts. Also, they can get distracted easily by anything passing in front of their eyes. As we will discuss later, visual elements are quite handy to attract their attention. These could be charts, photographs, and drawings. They might also be more interested in the clothes you're wearing or any gesture that you're doing involuntary. Because of this reason, you need to make a strong connection between what you are talking about and any visual material you're using (Duarte, 2010).

Kinesthetic learners are more likely to retain information by emotions. These people remember just a little piece of what they hear, but they will recall exactly how they feel about something. For example, you may have an experience wherein you said something in a neutral voice to a colleague, friend, or relative, and they seem to have forgotten about it a little afterward. However, if you angrily scream to them and make them feel bad, the chances of them recalling what you say increase. You may even remember a situation in which you're very joyful, sad, or irritated and recall very well what made you feel that way.

A kinesthetic brain works that way. Consequently, a smart strategy is to focus on the emotions that your speech could provoke. What is the desired reaction to your speech? Maybe you're making a sales pitch and you need people to feel excited about your product or service. Focus on the benefits and make them clear how thrilled they'll be after getting it. Or maybe you're trying to raise awareness about a matter that concerns you. The feeling you could target is distress. Make clear what the consequences are if action is not taken today.

Body Language

Your body language and overall appearance are other features that you need to take care of. A good share of all communication depends entirely on our physical presence. Unconsciously, our minds decide whether we're going to take seriously somebody based on how we perceive them superficially (Ekman, 2003). Obviously, there are so many things that we unknowingly do. Nevertheless, there are a number of ways of taking control of our body.

Body language itself is a topic that is worth writing an entire book about. Nonetheless, we'll focus on the four key factors.

Posture

Shoulders back, back straight, always looking to the front. That's the natural position for our bodies to be in good balance. Be aware that posture is a sign of how comfortable we are in any situation. What is important here is that you don't go to any extreme. If you keep a posture where your body is bent forward, that will seem as if you lack confidence. On the other hand, having your chest and chin up may look as if you're trying to intimidate. The best way to go is to keep a relaxed and balanced posture.

If you have a problem with your posture, look for corrective exercises. Do it not only for the sake of body language in public speaking but also for protecting your back!

Eye Contact

It shouldn't come as a surprise that keeping subtle eye contact with people is a sign of honesty and transparency. Of course, it's almost impossible to keep eye contact with every single individual if you're speaking to 50 or more people in a room. There are tricks, though, to create the illusion that you are. If you feel uncomfortable looking into people's eyes when delivering a speech, you can imagine "invisible points" across the room. Every time you're staring at these points, it will produce the illusion that you're keeping eye contact with somebody.

As you move smoothly, also change slowly from one invisible point to the other. You don't need to stare at these points all the time. Look somewhere else and return your sight to these points. What's important here is that you keep things natural. Blink as you'd usually do.

Hand Gestures

"To receive everything, one must open one's hands and give," the Buddhist priest Taisen Deshimaru once proclaimed. Hands play a key role in letting people know what our actual intentions are. Specialists in body language suggest that hiding hands under the table or inside our pockets might be a red flag since it can be perceived that we have something else to hide besides our hands. At the same time, we should be sure that we're not over-gesticulating with your hands.

Move your hands softly to emphasize the important points of your speech. Hand gestures are important in storytelling. If you're referring to the Three Musketeers, you can raise three fingers. If you're speaking about a river, you can use your hands to replicate the flow of the water. Make sure that your hands are helping your audience to visualize your speech.

Movement

Going from one side of the room to the other every 15 seconds is a clear sign that you're nervous. People will quickly notice this. And you'll notice that they noticed. Before you can react properly, you're moving faster and even in shorter time-lapses. It's completely fine to move now and then, and it's even recommendable to do so. In front of a big audience, moving and standing in different positions will help you to keep an eye with most (if not all) of the people listening to you.

Consider anyhow that moving from one side to the other can help you to interact better with people. The key issue is to use movement in order to engage people with your speech. If you raise a question, you can move toward a part of the audience as if you were looking for the answer among them.

Always face the audience and never give your back. The movement of your body should go with the flow of your speech to show that you're open to the audience. Movement is an excellent way to show that you're receptive to people. So use your body movement as an invitation for people to interact with you.

Outfits

Last but not least, in this subject, you don't want your superb body language to be spoiled by a terrible outfit. When choosing clothes, don't think, "How do I look?" but "What messages am I sending?" (Shulman, 2001). A conservative and elegant suit will immediately send an authority message. A more casual outfit will make people perceive that you're an approachable person and that you prefer horizontal communication instead of a hierarchical one. And naturally, an extravagant choice of colors and clothes will make the audience take everything you say with a grain of salt. However, if empathy is what you intend to achieve, it's wise to mirror your audience's outfits. Take that into consideration if you're giving a speech at your local community.

Visual Materials

Few people know how to use visual materials properly during a speech. I'm sure that you have (at least once) watched any of the following situations:

The speaker opens a PowerPoint file, and there are way too many slides. Halfway through the presentation, the speaker realizes little time is left. The speaker starts rushing and saying, "I'll just show you some few important pictures," while just jumping most of the slides that originally were at the PowerPoint file.

What about when the speaker decides to write a wall of text on the slides and you're not sure if you should follow what the speaker says, try to read everything on the wall of text, or simply ignore everything altogether.

Here's a piece of advice: less is more. When using visual materials, the key is to be resourceful (Duarte, 2010). Keep in mind that the star of the show must be you, not the PowerPoint slide. It isn't rare to find speakers who try to use visual resources to compensate for the lack of content in their speeches. Certainly, visual materials are a great tool, but they should be used as something to help you illustrate a point, not to be the point itself.

Before using visual materials, think about whether you really need them. Does talking about the topic alone provide the big picture, or do you need something visual to accomplish that? If visual materials are needed, start looking at what can help you to illustrate your point better.

Here are two clear examples of what I mean:

You may be describing something that is visually complex. Describing every single detail of it is time-consuming; thus, a picture can facilitate the audience to see what you are talking about.

You may be talking about how something develops in time and space (for example, economic growth). You might speak about percentages and numbers. People need context and relativity to understand the relevance of what you're speaking. Thus, you use graphs and tables to make your point come across.

So when do you not use visual materials?

Avoid visual materials when speaking about something generic. Why would you waste time explaining how a cup of tea or how a chair looks like? If you're certain that your mental picture coincides with the one of your audience, there's no need to illustrate it further.

Don't use visual materials when the focus has to be in you. Often, speakers feel the need to switch pictures and slides every time they come up with a different argument. Figure out when the audience has to pay attention exclusively to you and visual materials are not needed.

Don't use visual materials without first making sure how they would look like during the actual speech. A PowerPoint presentation might look incredible in your computer, but it might not be the case when projected by a beamer. Try to test before your presentation to see you how it looks like.

Don't use PowerPoint slides exclusively. I'm not an enemy of PowerPoint. My point here is that you shouldn't limit yourself to this software. There are several other options out there that are quite impressive (give a look to Prezi, for example). A further alternative is to use non-technological visual materials. What if you speak about food? Bring some of it for the audience to enjoy! Music? Play some songs for the audience. Use your imagination in this one.

Invite Your Audience to Use Their Imagination

But what if you are in a circumstance where you can't use visual materials? At this point, you should have noticed that I repeatedly use hypothetical examples to illustrate the points discussed in each chapter. There's a good reason for that. The resources in this book might be limited, and you must take advantage of any element that can play in your favor. In this case, instead of flooding your audience with images, you can ask them to use their imagination to explain a concept.

Imagination is a powerful tool. When people use it, they generate mental images to describe a concept in terms that are familiar to them (Duarte, 2010). If I ask you to imagine a house, a school, or a park, you're likely to recreate them in your mind as they are in the place where you live. In the very same way, when you ask your audience to imagine something to illustrate a concept, they will be able to put everything in terms that they are acquainted with.

Recap

Now, let's do something interesting with our mind experiment. What I want you to do is to practice your speech. Do it in your bedroom or wherever you feel the most comfortable. Set your timer and try to deliver your speech in less than 10 minutes. On top of that, record yourself delivering the speech.

When you deliver your speech, pretend that you're before an actual audience. Speak as you'll speak to the people listening to you. This might be a strange thing to do, but becoming a great public speaker is just like becoming a great sportsman. Constant practice is necessary!

Once you're done, see the recording. Notice every single aspect we discussed in this chapter. Take note of your body language, your voice, and how you used visual materials (if you decided to use them at all). Once you're done with this, make a list of the things that you'd improve and study them.

Record yourself again and try improving the way you delivered the speech. Repeat this process as many times as it is necessary. The final point is that you end with a version of your speech that makes you feel satisfied and that you'd be confident to present.

Don't hesitate to show these recordings to a friend or relative who can give you a fair opinion and constructive feedback. If you're comfortable with this, you'll certainly get some insights that you might have missed otherwise. Use that criticism seriously and include it in the list of things to improve.

Chapter 11: Talking With Any One

Talking to people easily and without difficulty presupposes a common ground. And for that, it is essential to know for what reasons the interlocutor and you seek to communicate, to find bridges between these various motivations. This land will allow you to talk about your differences, find solutions, and allow you to be more creative together. If you do this with your entourage, people will want to listen to you and do what you offer them. Here are six simple techniques to find common ground to communicate with everyone.

1. Learn to feel what the other person is feeling rather than making others understand how you feel

When you talk to someone you've just met, it's essential to get people where they are! Depending on that, you will be able to direct them where you want.

Wherever you go, stay in touch with others, meet new people, and stay connected to others at all levels, regardless of age or status. From the largest to the smallest, do not forget anyone. Speak with everyone to create common ground! The inventor Charles F. Kettering said: "To know, it is very different to understand." So you have to get to know the points of view of those around you, from the chief executive to the security guard, take the trouble to talk to everyone to experience what others feel so that they follow you willingly. If you want to create a common ground, always start with what the other feels.

2. Learn to see what the other person is seeing rather than making one's own point of view

Many of us make the big mistake of wanting to share their way of seeing things often. We are continually trying to force everyone to adopt our personal vision. Even worse, we assume that it is acquired. When Paul Rees, at a leadership convention, was asked what he would do if he could go back in time, he said, "If I could go back to when I was a dad, I would try to see things according to their perspectives."

It is essential to take the situations from the point of view of your interlocutor rather than make them adopt yours.

3. Learn to keep abreast of what others know rather than to let others know

When you sit beside people to settle conflicts, you will realize that they only want to tell things through their personal feelings. They want to use this way to make themselves better understood. When you conflict, let others "empty their bags" without answering until they know the problem. Abraham Lincoln said, "When I'm getting ready to argue with someone, I spend a third of my time thinking about myself and what I'm going to say, and the other two-thirds thinking about him and what he will say. It should be inspired if you want to connect easily.

We can know a person well, but not understand it at all. We can likewise see a ray on a subject without understanding much. To follow someone, one must discern what he wants, and this requires going beyond the stage of the intellectual and understanding the heart of the person.

To conclude this message, here are some easy questions to better understand the state of mind of someone around you: "What are you dreaming about?" "What kind of song do you sing?" "What makes you cry?"

4 Project Absolute Confidences.

Another thing you must know is to talk to people with confidence. Being confident with your words can make even the most skeptical person believe in you. Speak with full conviction and certainty.

Even if you're not naturally confident, believe in yourself and act "as if" you're already the self-assured person you desire to be.

If you have a speech ready, make sure to rehearse a lot. You don't have to memorize every word, but you do have to be comfortable in what you're saying.

5 Know Your Audience.

Based on the psychology of communication, you should also find out just who you're talking to. What demographic do they belong to? Are they mostly men or women? Are students or professionals?

These details are very important and yet often overlooked. While your message might remain the same, the words you use and the way you express it must be tailor-fitted to your audience to achieve maximum results.

For example, everyone needs to know about tips on how to stay healthy every day. Most kids won't really understand the concept of antibodies, but they can understand what it means to be strong and have unlimited energy. It's all about customization; so do your research well.

6 Use Visual Effects.

Listening to someone talk and talk for hours can put any person to sleep. The psychology of communication suggests that you accompany your talks with visual effects.

These could be in the form of hand gestures and full-body movements. Teachers like to move around a lot so the students aren't just looking at the exact same point for an hour. They also like to use a lot of non-verbal approaches like hand gestures and facial expressions.

If you're talking about numbers, you need to prepare a powerpoint presentation or video to keep the whole discussion diverse.

So you can apply these few tracks to improve your daily conversations.

Chapter 12: How To Use The Principles Of Persuasion

In 1984, Dr. Robert B. Cialdini wrote a book called, "Influence: The Psychology of Persuasion." In this work, he shows how a person can use six different principles to develop communication skills in order to influence the actions of others. These six principles are:

Reciprocity

Consistency

Social Proof

Sympathy/Like-ability

Authority

Scarcity

He developed this system mainly for marketing purposes, but it can be used in almost every aspect of life. We will go through each step in more detail in this chapter.

Reciprocity

Reciprocity is the idea of tit for tat; you have to give some to get some. The way it works in marketing is by offering things such as free samples to your target audience in order to get them to come back for more. This principle can be applied in everyday life as well. By doing an unprovoked favor for someone, you build up a kind of credit with them. Knowing you did this thing for them, they are more likely to return the favor and help you out. It is a true example of you get what you give, that putting in the work will lead to the reward. This kind of communication and interaction can be very rewarding for both parties.

Consistency

Consistency and commitment seem to go hand in hand. The basic idea behind this principle is always being there. Doing what you say you are going to; staying committed to you word and consistent in your actions. In terms of marketing, it is often used to get higher conversion rates. The idea is that a person who buys a multitude of smaller, lower-priced items might be willing to commit to a similar, higher-priced item either now or at a later date.

Social Proof

Social proof is the idea that things good enough for everyone else are also good enough for me. It works by offering reviews or seeing people flock to a certain product. If two similar products are offered, but one seems to be selling out more quickly, the social proof would show that the faster selling item is of better quality or a better deal. Groups or sub-groups doing things will lead us to 'keep up with the Jones' and go for the products that others have proven to us are better. This can be used outside the marketing arena by seeing how a person interacts with a group of friends. Clearly, the person that captivates the most people or is able to keep more of the attention is the one you would be more apt to want to be around.

Sympathy/Like-ability

This is perhaps the most superficial principle of the six. It is the idea that we are more apt to do or buy something because we like it. We want to hang out with people because they look appealing. This entire principle can come down to something simple as an image. Sympathy, on the other hand, can be used to make people feel. It plays on the emotions to get things from others. You see a commercial with a bunch of starving kids and you feel horror or sadness at their situation. Then a man comes on TV asking for you to donate money to save these poor starving souls. They are trading your feelings for money and, in an attempt to assuage some feelings of guilt for living so much better than others, some people will give in and send money.

Authority

We are programmed to respect authority. We are taught to obey those in a position of authority and strive to be like them. Therefore, we are more apt to want to do what they do or tell us to do. This is the basic principle behind celebrity endorsement, this and like-ability. For instance, the better an athlete is, the more ads and commercials you will see him in. Why is this? Because he (or she) is the undisputed authority in their field. They are looked up to and respected and we want to eat and wear the same things they do. It is simply a part of human nature to look up to and respect those in authority. If you find that you have a celebrity or an authority figure that uses your product or leaves a solid review of your services, you want to put that information where people will see it. They are apt to decide that if it is good enough for (insert athlete here) then it is good enough for me.

Scarcity

We all know this one. "While supplies last." We hear it often. The idea behind this one is that if it is scarce or rare, we want it. If everyone can get it, that does not interest us as much. Being one of the only people to experience or own a certain product is a huge selling point for us because it plays into our need to be unique and individual. By using this simple phrase, companies are able to send people into a semi-panic mode causing them to go out and purchase whatever it is they are selling because they are sure to run out of stock soon. It is a genius-marketing tactic, really.

Now that we are more familiar with how to network ourselves and how to use the six principle of persuasion, it is time to find out how to use these skills to our advantage in our business lives.

Chapter 13: Psyche Up

Fear is all in the mind. No matter how much preparation you do, if you'll consistently tell yourself you cannot do it, or people will laugh at you, or there's no point in doing it, your fear and anxiety of public speaking will never go away.

If you'll ask Donald Trump why you have to overcome your public speaking anxiety, he'll tell you because it pays to do so, literally. And guess what, it pays handsomely. Many motivational speakers travel all around the world, receive huge checks and sell millions of copies of their books just by speaking in front of people, and getting great at it. Even business tycoons sell their leaderships to expand their organizations.

Imagine the millions of lives you can change if you'll take art of public speaking all the way. Imagine your life changing. If you'll consult a psychologist to help you with your fear right now, you will most probably be advised to imagine so many things. That's just how it works. You fear starts with an imagination, so it needs to end that way.

Picture yourself alone until you grow old simply because you can't even muster the courage to speak with other people, with strangers you barely know. Do you think that's fun? Would you rather grow and die alone than fight that fear today?

Picture yourself getting stuck on your career level – no promotions, below average salary, a "nobody" in the organization. Will you still be proud of your achievement? Do you think your fear took you somewhere else higher?

Picture yourself constantly getting ridiculed because you can't face the public decent enough to act normal. Do you think that will end anytime soon if you'll do nothing to change that?

Public speaking is an art, an art that is either innate or developed. It is either you are a natural motivator – a persuader – or one that has climbed his way through by studying and working hard to be the best. There's really no excuse not to be good at it, unless you don't really want to. And that's the biggest problem.

No help matters, no help is good enough if you won't accept it and start with helping yourself.

Chapter 14: Gestures

A gesture is a specific corporal movement that reinforces a verbal message or conveys a particular thought or emotion. Although the gestures must be done with:

º Head.

º Shoulders.

º Legs and feet.

º Most are made with hands and arms.

Hands can become excellent communication tools when speaking. But many speakers with little experience do not know what to do with their hands. Some try to get rid of them their own way by putting them in their pockets or placing them behind their backs. Some unconsciously release nervous tension by making awkward movements that distract attention. Some speakers make too many gestures because of the nerves, violently moving arms and hands.

To be effective, the gestures of the speaker must have meaning, even if they are performed unconsciously. They must be visible to the public. They must mean the same to the public as they do to the speaker. And they should reflect what is being said, as well as the full meaning of the message.

4.1.- WHY DO WE GESTICULATE?

All good speakers gesticulate. Why? Gestures are probably the most evocative form of non-verbal communication a speaker can use. No other physical action can improve your speech in as many ways as gestures do. Gestures:

º Clarify and support words. They reinforce the public's understanding of your verbal message.

º They bring drama to ideas. Along with words, gestures help to create vivid images in the minds of the audience.

º They provide emphasis and vitality to spoken discourse. Transmit your feelings and attitudes more clearly than your words.

º They help dissipate nervous tension in the speaker. Meaningful gestures serve as an outlet for natural nervous energy during the presentation of a speech.

º They work as visual tools. Increase attention and retention of the public.

º Encourage public participation. They help you indicate the answer you are looking for in your listeners.

º They have great visibility. They provide visual support when you address a large number of people and the audience can not see your eyes.

4.2.- TYPES OF GESTURES

Despite the vast number of movements that could be described as gestures, they can all be grouped into one of the following main categories:

DESCRIPTIVE GESTURES

Clarify or enrich the verbal message. They help the audience to understand the comparisons and contrasts, and to visualize the size, shape, movement, location, function and number of objects.

EMPHATIC GESTURES

Emphatic gestures underline your words. They indicate seriousness and conviction. For example, a closed fist suggests a strong feeling, such as anger or determination.

SUGGESTIVE GESTURES

Suggestive gestures symbolize ideas and emotions. They help the communicator to create a specific environment or express a specific thought.

Having an open palm suggests giving or receiving, usually an idea, while shrugging indicates ignorance, perplexity or irony.

INCITING GESTURES

The inciting gestures are used to evoke a desired response from the audience. If you want your listeners to raise their hands, applaud or perform a special action, you will get that answer by doing it as an example.

Gestures performed above the shoulders suggest physical height, inspiration or emotional exaltation.

Gestures made below the shoulders indicate rejection, apathy or condemnation.

Those that are performed at shoulder or near level suggest calmness and serenity.\

The most frequently used gesture is usually the open hand stretched towards the audience. The meaning of this type of gesture depends on the position of the hand. If it is held up, it means giving or receiving, although this gesture is sometimes used unconsciously, without any specific meaning. A hand down can express suppression, secrecy, completion or stability. If the palm of the hand is directed towards the audience it suggests high, repulsion, denial or aversion. If the hand is perpendicular to the speaker's body, it tends to suggest restraint, limits in space or time, comparisons or contrasts. Gestures reflect the individual personality of each speaker. What works for one speaker does not necessarily has to work for another.

However, the following six rules apply to anyone who wants to be a dynamic and effective communicator.

1.- React naturally to what you think, feel and say when presenting a speech. Express yourself in a natural way through gestures. Regardless of our personality or cultural background, we all have a natural urge to emphasize and reinforce words with gestures.

2.- Do not copy the gestures of another person, be authentic and spontaneous.

3.- If you impose artificial gestures to your natural style, the audience will realize and catalog you as a false person.

4.- Some people are animated naturally, while others are reserved.

5.- If you move your hands naturally and freely when speaking in an informal situation, move them in the same way when you present a speech.

6.- If you are a reserved and calm person, do not change your personality to adjust it to situations in which you have to speak in public.

4.3.- ACTION

Verbal and visual messages must act together to communicate the same thought or feeling. When a speaker does not match his gestures with his words, the result will be cardboard, artificial and, sometimes, even funny. Every gesture you make must have a purpose and reflect your words. In this way your listeners will perceive the effect instead of the gesture. Make sure that the strength and frequency of your gestures are appropriate for your words.

Make energetic and emphatic gestures only when you feel that the message requires it. From time to time you will have to adapt your gestures to the size and nature of the audience. In general terms, when the audience is large, your gestures should be broader and slower. Also keep in mind that a young audience will be attracted to communicators who use forceful gestures, but older and more conservative groups may consider annoying or threatening physical actions too energetic. The gestures you make during a speech will also be subject to the distribution of the audience. If you speak from a physically limited position, the broad and extensive gestures will be reduced. A typical example of a physically limited position is a main table with the audience sitting near the speaker.

4.4.- CONVINCE

Your gestures should be animated and varied if you want them to convey the impression you want. A gesture that is half done suggests that the speaker does not have enough conviction and momentum. Every gesture made with the hand should be a complete body movement that starts from the shoulder, never from the elbow. Move the whole arm away from the body, with ease and simplicity. Keep your wrists and fingers relaxed, never rigid or tense. Good gesticulation is strong enough to convince, but it must be done slowly and widely to be seen clearly. The gestures should be varied but not irregular, they should never follow an established pattern.

Any gesture has three parts: preparation, travel and return. During the preparation your body begins to move in anticipation of the gesture itself. The route is the gesture itself and the return makes your body recover a balanced position to speak.

The movement of the gesture (balance, preparation, travel, return, recover balance) must be done smoothly so that only the travel is visible to the audience. Just as knowing when to say something is a key element for comedians, knowing when to make a gesture is as important as the quality of it. The -travel- must be produced in the exact word at the exact time, neither before nor after. However, the preparation can start long before the travel; in fact, it can have a striking effect by starting the second before and then maintaining the attention until the exact moment of the travel. The return supposes, simply, to drop your hands gently on each side and does not have to be a quick movement. Do not try to memorize gestures and incorporate them into the speech. Memorized gestures tend to go badly because the speaker helps himself by the word whose gesture should be used to emphasize it. The result is that the gesture follows the word, making it look artificial and clumsy.

Turn your natural and spontaneous gestures into a habit. The first step to become an expert in gesturing is to recognize what gestures you usually make.

BODY MOVEMENT

Changing your position or location during a speech, is the most general and visible form of physical action that, as a communicator, you can perform. But this can be a great advantage or a huge disadvantage depending on the way you would like to present your speeches. When you move your whole body in a controlled and determined manner during a speech, you get three advantages.

To begin with, body movement can support and reinforce your words. And, of course, the movement will almost always attract the attention of the audience. Finally, body movement is the fastest and most effective way to release anxiety and relieve physical tension.

All these characteristics can also, however, turn against you. A rule to make body movement your ally and not your enemy is this: never move without a reason. The gaze is directed, inevitably, towards moving objects and that is why any bodily movement during a speech attracts attention. If you accompany your movements with your verbal message, you will stimulate the attention and receptivity of the audience while enriching your speech. Looking at an immobile object is boring, so do not stay fixed in the same place while talking. On the other hand, body movement should be controlled by moderation. Too much movement, even if done correctly, can distract the audience. The idea is to find a middle point that consists of enough movement to keep the attention of the listeners but without distracting them from the speech. In the same way that intentional movements attract attention, so do random movements. The body will do practically anything to release tension. Unperceived speakers perform movements such as wiggling, swaying or taking steps without realizing that they are doing it. If talking in public makes you nervous and tense, try to incorporate enough useful movements in your speeches so that your body does not make unconscious gestures that distract attention.

EXERCISE:

Never do this with your body when speaking in public:

While your movements are natural and almost automatic, you must be on the lookout to avoid the most common mistakes. I recommend you avoid doing the following at all costs:

º Avoid putting your hands in your pockets.

º Avoid touching your face with your hands while you are in front.

º Avoid swinging from side to side for no reason.

º Avoid joining your hands to the front or crossing them.

º Avoid hiding your hands behind your back or your head.

º Avoid forced and unnatural movements.

How much will you need to practice?

Have patience with yourself, because you will have to practice all these aspects several times in order to correct them.

Remember that the vast majority of our body movements are automatic and unconscious. That is why, once you become aware of them, you will need constant repetition to turn that automatic body language into a more positive and appropriate one, while the automatic part is something that you can not change.

Learn to use your body to reinforce what your words say, and NEVER to contradict you. Put into practice what you just learned from today, and you will experience positive results.

Chapter 15: Putting It All Together

Now that you have written your speech, planned your outfit, practiced your gestures, movements and delivery, you are ready to face your audience as a public speaker. This last chapter will give you tips that you can apply while you are speaking. In this chapter, you will learn how to put all the elements of a good speech and speaker together to make your audience listen to and understand what you are trying to say.

Smile!

Don't frown or sulk unless the situation calls for it. Smile, grin and laugh. Don't be afraid to be completely at ease with the stage or podium and with your audience. Warm, jolly speakers help the crowd gravitate to them and their message. Plus, smiling will help keep the tension at bay and will allow you to feel more confident about your speech.

Remember: You practiced for this.

You put time, hard work and effort into preparing for your public speech. Allow yourself to reap the rewards of your work. Speak to your audience just like you practiced. Don't worry if you miss some words or mispronounce a few syllables. Continue speaking with passion and determination. The limelight is turned on you and you deserve it.

Improvise

There will be times when unexpected events call for ingenious improvisation on your part. Relax. You'll be fine as long as you remember the basic lessons every good speaker clings to: Confidence, Charisma, and Knowledge. If you are grounded in those three concepts, then improvisation or ad lib will come naturally to you.

Work the Room

Go around. Get near your audience. Let them interact with you. You are not a public speaker if you do not have any listeners. Let your audience feel that they are important; that you are speaking on their behalf as much as yours. Treat the audience as you would a friend and you will find that public speaking is as easy as talking to the people you know really well.

Chapter 16: Find Common Ground And Find It Fast.

I speak about entrepreneurship at high schools from time to time. High school students love to throw things. Sometimes, they throw things at me. One time, a tampon hit the whiteboard while I presented. I am not kidding. It almost hit me in the head. I wondered why teenagers are fascinated with throwing things so I experimented. I realized when I was in a suit and tie and used big words, there was a higher likelihood objects would be thrown. As soon I took off my jacket, loosened up my tie, and dropped a bit of urban slang, they stopped throwing things. Some of them even listened. Well, I think they listened. At least they stopped throwing things at me. I now take off my jacket and loosen my tie in the first two minutes of the presentation. Turns out, this makes a big difference.

Even if you are not speaking to high school students, the level of audience engagement during your entire speech depends on the first two minutes. If you want to win over your audience right away, relate to them from the beginning of your presentation.

The highest level of anxiety and uncertainty most often occurs in the first two minutes of a presentation. This is true for both the speaker and the audience. The audience comes to the meeting or event wanting you to succeed, but they will decide in the first couple of minutes if they like you and if they will remain engaged. This explains, at least in part, why speakers are weary of their first 120 seconds on stage. Speakers fear the "all eyes on me" piece of presenting. They feel immense pressure to entertain their audience and capture their attention with witty banter or jokes that may or may not flop. I am here to tell you there is an easier way to engage your audience from the start. There is a way to make them listen and feel more comfortable. It is basically the same as taking off your suit jacket, loosening your tie, and dropping some urban slang.

You already did the heavy lifting. You know what they want to learn. Now your job becomes showing them why you are the right person to teach. If you can get the audience to think, "He or she is one of us" in the first two minutes of your presentation, you have won. Your job just got 100 times easier. You don't have to be nervous that you will forget your opening jokes or scripted lines. You don't even need scripted lines or jokes. You just spend the first two minutes telling a story. Your story. The one that shows your audience you were once in their exact seat. You share common ground, similar struggles and obstacles, and seek the same solution. They want to know that it was not always easy for you. Before you can provide hope, you must share your struggle. Smug superiority is not effective. We have all been at speeches where the speaker puts himself or herself on a pedestal as someone who has all the answers. I have trouble connecting with this style of speaking. You probably do, too. So does your audience. A story of struggle on the other hand, is relatable. You must do it in the first 120 seconds. Here is an effective example of finding common ground.

The director of a sales team started the presentation with, "I know it's tough out there. I remember being a salesperson myself and understand the challenges that come with the role. I struggled to make my numbers, sometimes for months at a time. On more than one occasion, I was almost fired because my sales were so low. I felt hopeless. I knew I was a good salesperson, but did not know how to improve my situation. One day, I figured out a three-part formula that worked. It was almost like magic. I tested these principles, and within six weeks became one of the top salespeople in my entire company. If you feel hopeless, or know you can produce more than your current output reflects, then I hope these three principles will serve you, too."

Well done, Sales Director. Your audience is ready to listen to you as a public speaker.

When I train a group of speakers who want to monetize their message, I share my story about getting my own speaking career started. At the beginning of my career, I self-organized speeches so I could practice. I begged my friends to come. I bought them wine. I bought them a lot of wine. I was almost broke several times in the first 18 months. A few weeks away from being flat broke for a third time, Google offered me a job. I did not even apply for a job at Google. They found me and made me an offer. A good offer. I thought about taking it. I wanted the free food and bicycles that Google provided its employees. I wanted financial security. Appealing as it sounded, Google wasn't my dream. I told their paycheck and their food and bicycles, "No." It felt good. But I was still broke. I started doing things differently in my business and gained momentum. I tracked the changes and noticed five specific strategies resulted in increased income, opportunity, and exposure. I tested this theory and a year later generated a six-figure speaking business. I now train my audience on the exact five strategies I used.

After I take my audience through this first 120 seconds, they are all ears. They want to learn what worked for me. They are hungry to deliver a message. They are in the same spot I was three years ago. They may be broke. They may be tired of self-organizing talks. They may be tired of buying wine so people come hear them speak. They may not know what to do next. This makes the following 30 minutes of training exciting for the audience and me. This will be true for your presentation as well. Remember, the level of audience engagement during your entire speech depends on the first two minutes.

Relate to them early. Relate to them fast. Relate to them often.

Chapter 17: Heart Link: The Voice As An Instrument

"We often refuse to accept an idea merely because the tone of the VOICE in which it has been expressed is unsympathetic to us."

– Friedrich Nietzsche

On February 9th 2012, I was in Kampala, Uganda. I had been invited for the second time to deliver a speech to the Eastern Africa Youth Conference organized by an international organization known as Initiative of Change (IOFC). The conference had delegates from the Eastern Africa region. It also had other guests from Cameroon, the United States of America

and Nepal.

The speakers invited came from all across these countries with

a background in politics, leadership, business and academics. My

topic was "accountability and values", and when my time came

to take to the stage I knew exactly what I wanted to deliver and

how to deliver it. Within the thirty minutes of my speech I had

captured the momentum, engaged the audience with passion and

delivered my volleys home. At the end of the speech, the entire

room rose to give me a standing ovation.

During the questions and answer session, I remember one

Southern Sudanese lady, a daughter of a government minister,

who took the privilege to comment on my speech. She really

struggled to get the words to describe my speech as she said

"This is it, I like this, I mean the power, the voice and the way

speaker released it with all force ... this is the way it should be!"

The entire room applauded her for the comment. When I was

handling a workshop on public speaking in the same conference,

one leader of the group from Kenya commented, "The speech was

so powerful, you delivered it with such passion that even if you

were lying to us, we would still believe the lies".

The voice is the core of public speaking and the defining factor of communication. As a trained musician, I know that the voice

from the Heart

is an instrument. It is said that public speaking is nine-tenths

voice work and that a rich correctly used voice is the greatest

physical factor of persuasiveness and power, often over-topping

the effects of reason. That is, if a person uses his or her voice well

Public Speaking

in sharing something to you, you might find yourself persuaded

-

to believe them without reasoning what they have just said.

Dan Mugera

Personal culture

A good voice does not just exist; you have to work it out. A good voice is a mark of personal culture developed over a period. Let me

ask you, how do you normally talk to people? Are you a student of

human nature or are you a student of life? Majority of us live life simply expecting good things including

a good voice without being aware that life does not give you what

you deserve but what you demand from it. A good voice is an effective possession for the professional

speaker and it could also be a great commercial asset as we have

seen all over the world. However, it does not end there because

one needs to be aware and develop this culture. Some people

talk rudely to others and still expect that when they go on stage they will all of a sudden gain that magic voice to draw people to

them. Forget it. Some people do not take time to be friendly to

others and still expect that when they get to the office they will

have a passionate voice when doing a speech. You simply throw

a general "hey guys" to your colleague, go to your desk and get

immersed to work and then when you go on stage, that becomes

the time for rehearsals instead of time for doing the real thing.

If you want to have a voice that people will listen to, change

your personal culture. Begin by taking time to greet people with

curiosity. Look at somebody in the eyes as you shake their hands

passionately and ask, "How are you doing?" "How is life and your family?" When people detect that you are interested in them as

a person, they will be interested to listen. Take time to listen to

people without judging them. You cannot have a good voice if

your heart is full of hate, rage and malice. It cannot be possible

if all that you do with your voice, ninety percent of the time is

backbiting, back stabbing, manipulation, slander, deceit, and

condemnation. You need to change these habits in your life.

Purpose to use your voice to love, adore, encourage, support,

care, motivate, lead, correct, transform, build and cherish, and you

will realize how addictive and compounding this will become.

You will begin to be magnetic and wherever people hear your

voice even if you are talking nothing really of importance, people

will want to listen. This will help in creating a personal culture

in developing the carrying power of the voice as we are going to

find out in this chapter.

I concur with Gladstone observation that, "Ninety men in

every hundred in the crowded professions will never rise above mediocrity

because the training of the voice is entirely neglected and considered of no

importance".

I have realized the truth of the above words said by Gladstone

many years ago as I have listened to speakers, executive

presentations, news anchors and reporters many times. Perhaps one of the places where people also miss in the handling of their

voice is during times of interviews. I have had the opportunity

to sit in interviewing panels and prepare senior executives who

were going to face an interviewing panel and I have discovered

people always invest a lot on the basics of the interview without

putting in mind the importance of the voice in convincing the

panels of their qualifications for the job. One day, a lady and a

- chief magistrate, came to me for training in public speaking. It

was just a few weeks to the 'grand' vetting and interviewing of the High Court judges of Kenya according to the new judiciary

reform laws stipulated in the new constitution which was

promulgated in 2010. I took her through training and emphasized

the need for substance, audibility, passion and sense of occasion

when speaking. Whenever she could stand to speak before me,

I would stress on tone variation, eye contact and energy in her

voice. She went ahead and did the interview which was live on

major television stations in Kenya and was endorsed as successful

to become one of the new high court judges in Kenya.

Later, the person who had referred the lady to me who has also

passed through our training called me even before I had known the lady had qualified and told me gladly "Dan, this thing of yours

works man, the lady is now one of the new judges in Kenya!" I

called the lady to congratulate her and she told me, "Dan thanks,

this victory is for all of us."

You cannot as a speaker neglect the training of the voice.

Recently another executive came to me; he had come all the

way from Western Kenya to do training in public speaking in

Nairobi. He had been referred to me by his sister, a student of

mine. During training I learnt that he was a Managing Director

of a major parastatal and he was about to go for an interview

seeking to be promoted to become a chief executive of another major parastatal within the same line of career.

As we went through the training, I noted that audibility was

one of his major problems which he confirmed to be true. You

could barely hear him when speaking yet he was just a few meters

away. We took the opportunity to work on his projection, tone

variation and energy in his voice as well as other key ingredients of

public speaking and especially how to face an interviewing panel.

I emphasized to him my philosophy of facing an interviewing

panel which is 'relaxation', I told him that it was not a do or die

affair, that he should face the panel and enjoy himself. If he gets

the job then he should celebrate and if not, it is not the end of the world. He did that and passed the interview. You should have

heard him when he called me in excitement to deliver the good

news. Since then, whenever he is going to deliver any speech, he

will first consult me even if it is on the phone to ask me for some

tips on how to do it better.

What then are the keys to a good voice?

The keys to a good voice are;

- Relaxation.
- Openness.
- Projection.
- Charm.

These I want to believe will bring about the element of having a

from the Heart

good voice and enhance the mark of a personal culture. You need to master relaxation because it is the secret of a good voice. You

should never force your tones because as an instrument, the voice

is delicate. You need to practice and allow your voice to move

Public Speaking

and not to force it move. This will help you stay away from any

• unnatural constriction which can harm your voice.

Dan Mugera

Before and when on stage, always learn to whisper to yourself

"relax, take it ease," and make sure your entire system relaxes so

that your voice will sound relaxed. Does it surprise you that any

time a man or woman goes on stage and he/she is not relaxed, you will definitely hear it in his voice? Why? Because the voice is the

medium of communication.

We cannot possible conclude the subject of relaxing without

talking about breathing. Majority of people have not learned the

proper way to breathing especially when delivering a speech. No

wonder you will hear breathing sounds in between sentences

when some speakers are speaking. You must always breathe from

your diaphragm; it is the natural and correct method of breathing.

Never try to breathe through your throat, breath the right way

and you will find yourself relaxed.

Another key to a good voice is openness. Many people do

not like opening their mouths wide and this hinders them from

molding beautiful tones when speaking. It is said that sound is a

series of waves and for you to produce great sounds; you have to

open your mouth wide. The voice which produces the sounds is

a series of air vibration and can only be strengthened with more

air and more vibration. You therefore need to learn to open your

mouth wide when speaking and punch the words well.

Vocal projection is very necessary in any delivery. A correctly

projected voice will definitely clear the throaty tones which most

of the times are inefficient, unattractive and harmful to the throat.

When you project your tone forward as you speak, you will be able to project it very well. It is this act of projection, which helps

you develop the carrying power of your voice a fit which is a mark

of distinction in all great speakers. You will realize that with

proper projection you do not necessarily need to speak loudly to

be heard at a distance but only to speak correctly.

For proper projection;

• Make sure your body posture is upright when speaking.

• Do not gaze at the floor when speaking.

• Renew you breathe after every moment.

• Do not force your voice when hoarse.

• Do not drink cold water when speaking; this will injure the

heated organs of speech.

• Avoid pitching your voice too high because it will become

raspy.

Practice the following syllables ascending and descending:

doh, re, me, fah, so, la, Te, doh're' me'

doh,re,me,re,me,fah,me,fah,so,fah,so,la,so,la,te,la,te,doh' te,doh're'me'

Once you master the above syllables interchange them with

the syllable 'la' and continue practicing projecting your voice.

Finally, another key factor to a good voice is what I call "vocal

from the Heart

charm". Have you ever been so attracted to a voice that you want

to continue listening even though you cannot tell why the voice

is so attractive? Vocal charm is the secret. Charm is a subtle

magnetism that is delightfully contagious. Speakers need to learn

Public Speaking

how to master this priceless gem for usage when engaging the

- audience and in their everyday lives.

Dan Mugera

Dale Carnegie observed that, "It is impossible to think selfishthoughts

and have an attractive personality, a lovely character, or a charming voice.

If you want to posses voice charm, cultivate a sincere sympathy for mankind.

Love will shine out through your eyes and proclaim itself in your tones. Your

character beautifies or mars your voice. As a man thinks in his heart so is his

voice".

What a powerful observation by Dale!

This is an eye-opener to anyone seeking to develop vocal

charm so as to draw people through his voice and influence them.

Remember that it is a process and you must be aware of your

surrounding and the lives of the people you seek to address for

you to find yourself applying this peculiar key in your life and

speaking.

Chapter 18: Identify Good Public Speakers

And Study How They Deliver

When I was taking public speaking, the tutor always encouraged us to watch videos of professional public speakers, especially politicians.

While most of us do not like politicians, one thing is clear; the better the speaker they are, usually the more success they have.

Some of the best politicians to observe are presidential candidates; again, this is not about your political opinion but simply learning effective skills from people that practice on a daily basis.

Your goal should be to take notes and then compare your video to theirs. One interesting tip is to actually write down part of the speech that the politician is giving, **and then you should try to emulate** the exact part or the entire speech and see how close you can get to a similar performance.

You want to notice things like, tone of their voice, body positioning which also accompanies spoken words, the kind of speech that they are giving for the content that they are delivering. Also note the kind of words that they use and pitch of their voice when they speak these words, as well as how they use emotions to convey thoughts. You also want to pay particular attention to gestures and stances and when.

Study Body Language

Body language is critical to delivering an effective speech. It does little good to have a great speaking voice but you do not take enough time to connect with the audience for proper body positioning and body language.

Try to take the opportunity to become a public speaking and body language expert because truly gifted public speakers understand that it is more than just the words they are speaking and seeking. A powerful and emotional presentation combined with the right gestures and body language can really make a huge difference when it comes to delivering a successful speech.

Part of study body language is to understand that even though you may rehearse for long periods of time, you want your speech to come across as natural and flowing as possible.

One of the best ways to prove that you are speaking from your heart is to ditch long pages of notes and simply have bulleted points that you have rehearsed, long before you step up to the podium. Use notes to cue your memory only.

The ultimate goal is to appear to be unrehearsed and natural but yet still having the cadence of information, persuasive speaking and emotional content that will convince others that you are not only intelligent, but wise and should be listened to and acted upon.

Never Lose Your Cool

One extremely important consideration is that you never lose your cool when speaking before an audience. Sometimes you can lose your cool because people want to argue with you or possibly heckle you during your speech.

Intelligent people understand that this is going to happen to them and have a contingency plan to deal with this situation. Here are a few simple rules you should follow so that you never lose your cool:

Restate the question or challenge - by restating the question or challenge that comes from the audience, you first show that you respect them enough to want to understand their point; when you do, restate what they are saying and keep it simple. Try to redefine what they are saying in a way that will allow you to respond to their questions with FACTS so you can make your point.

Ask questions BUT DO NOT ARGUE - one powerful technique that highly trained public speakers use is to ask questions in such a way so they can shape the narrative back to what they were saying. This also allows you to shape the discussion the way you see fit.

Provide only facts to the heckler / challenger — it is at this point that you've identified a weakness in what either the heckler or challengers are saying so you can now add facts to redirect back to the point of the speech.

Let me give you an example of this process.

Let's say you're discussing the importance of all Americans having the legal right to carry a firearm in a concealed fashion.

While you are giving your presentation someone stands up and says that this will increase the murder rate and fewer guns should be society's focus not more. How dare you!

It is at this point that you can be glad you have researched your speech. You can now point out that Uniform Crime Reports as issued by the FBI have shown a steady and large **decrease** in homicides as gun sales increase.

In places that do not allow concealed carry, have shown a steady and large decrease in homicides as gun sales increase; and places that do not allow concealed carry (i.e. gun free zones) tend to have the highest murder rates.

Now you can ask the question something like this – "Do the statistics show that we are safer or in more danger with more guns?" You then deliver FACTS and blow the heckler away, no pun intended.

This is all part of keeping your cool but without research and ready facts, this speech could turn into a disaster.

Also ALWAYS be as polite as possible as you are delivering a speech for everyone, not just the heckler.

Remember that keeping your cool also means that you are organized, well prepared, have an idea of how to deal with tough questions and possible hecklers.

Chapter 19: Speak From The Heart

How then do you proceed with the presentation? Should you speak like the head of an academic faculty addressing the students, or an official of government department telling citizens how they ought to conduct their affairs? If you are neither of the two persons above, the masters of the art of public speaking would recommend you adopt a conversational tone.

Speak to the people from the heart, with feelings and emotions, the way you would do to a family member or next door neighbour. Do not forget, the person you are talking to is actually someone's mother or brother and also someone's neighbour.

Do, please, address them as such, using homely words, to show you care about their feelings.

How would you achieve a conversational style of delivery? Well, like every other artistic skill, this too must be learned. Hardly was anyone born with the skill to speak in any particular manner, good or bad. Whatever style you now deploy, must have been learned over a period of time, consciously or otherwise.

Points to note

Use your own words.

While preparing your public speech, try to understand the topic so well that you can discuss it reasonably, without looking into a source material. Having a good understanding of the topic will bolster your self-confidence and help you to relax and speak as if to friends. Your talk will be engaging if you truly engage the audience with rhetorical questions that challenge them to be part of the conversation. This means that, even if you have a written paper to deliver, you'll frequently go off the books and say things in your words. Reading out facts and expressions, the way they appear in a printed text before you, will hardly give anyone the image of a great public speaker.

Read with feelings.

Granted, there are times when your presentation may demand that you actually read out a printed text. It may be a quote, which needs to be delivered verbatim. Where substantial materials are to be read out in full, masterful presentation means that you know the text so well as to read it with fluency and proper emotion.

Thus, you convey, not only the message of the text, but also the feelings that are intended by the author. If the text, for instance, has to do with things that make people healthy and happy, you endeavour to show the intended happiness in your face and tone. Of course, you cannot present facts about terrorism with a warm smile! Reference to bad news would call for a matching frown of rejection.

Engage the audience.

A relaxed mood is made clear when you focus on the audience while you speak. You only need to take brief moments to consult your outline. As you look into the audience, you may find it helpful to make eye contact with one person at a time, rather than just looking over the sea of human heads. Brief eye contacts with different people in the audience will give your talk a personal touch that would be lacking if you bury your eyes in the text, or keep looking over people's heads.

Beyond the eye contacts, your posture also matters. Good speakers pay attention to how they stand and move on the stage. They use facial expressions, gestures of the hand, head and body to attract and hold audience attention, motivating the audience to remain attentive and follow the conversation.

Bear in mind that your posture and sundry gestures, more than the message itself, can make the audience see you as warm and friendly. This, in turn, will help you achieve the overall objective of reaching their hearts and persuading them to act or think in the way that you recommend.

Avoid undue casualness, high drama

While a conversational or relaxed presentation is decidedly better in public talks, speakers do well to avoid undue casualness. Overly casual style has tendency of making a talk look unserious, unimportant and lacking in dignity. You'd sound so boring that listeners would opt out if they can, doze off or simply lose interest. In these days of ubiquitous hand held devices, a boring public talk tells the audience it's time to browse, text, chart, catch up on the emails and even watch favourite movies.

The other side of the coin, over dramatization, is also bad. A speaker may be carried away by the nature of a talk, or the urge to motivate people to action, that he veers off into undue drama. This can put many people off, or even divert attention from the message. So, by all means, you strive to speak with appealing tone and posture, while maintaining the

Chapter 20: The Very Best Way To Get Your Points Across

The main purpose of your public speaking event, is to improve the lives of your audience. You can only do that, if they understand and remember what you are teaching.

At the end of every talk, does the audience always go away with full understanding? Do they always remember everything they heard? Unfortunately the answer is no.

It's a shame. The speaker took time preparing the talk. The audience took time out to try and learn something that would improve their lives.

You need to deliver your talk in such a way that your audience understands all your points. Not only that, but you want them to remember. There is a very effective way of doing it.

The best way to get your audience to absorb and remember what you say is by telling stories. Stories do several things. They show something in action. They do an excellent job of explaining something and are the best way of helping people remember. They have been around for thousands of years. There's a very good reason. People love stories.

If you simply stand there and give facts and information, it's just lifeless. It isn't memorable.

Tell stories to make what you say come alive. It's the difference between telling someone a research method and actually giving them a demonstration.

By just giving information and facts, it will more likely be forgotten very quickly. However, if you use stories, then they will remember and understand.

To prove this point, I'll ask you a question. Do you remember the story of Goldilocks and the Three Bears? Do you recall the story of The Three Little Pigs? What about the story of The Wizard of Oz? I'm sure you have no trouble remembering these stories and many more like them.

Here's another question. When was the last time you heard these stories? I bet it's been a long time. However, you still remember them. Maybe you can't recite them word-for-word, but you would still be able to tell it in your own words.

As you can see, stories are memorable. This is one reason to use them. They are the best device to help your audience remember what you say in your public speaking event.

Another benefit of stories is that they demonstrate and teach things very well. Non-fiction book authors realise the power of stories to demonstrate and teach ideas.

I read a very good book several years ago. It was a book by an author called Robert Cialdini. He wrote a book about persuasion. It showed that there are six main techniques that people use on us to get us to do something.

His book is jam packed with stories. I still remember them and the points they taught.

Another very famous book is called, 'How to Win Friends and Influence People' by Dale Carnegie. This book outsold every other book except the Bible for a good ten years. It still sells today and it doesn't show any sign of stopping.

If you've ever read this book, you will notice the book is filled with many stories. All these stories are there for one purpose. They help you understand what the author is teaching.

I think you get the message by now. Use stories. They effectively teach your audience and they remember.

You may have noticed that I have used stories in this book. It's because they are the best way of helping you gain the most benefit.

What stories do you tell?

The best stories are the one's showing your own or other people's experiences. Essentially, true stories.

Try to always tell a true story. Don't make it up. If you do, your audience will spot it. The only difference to this rule, is if you explain that the story is made up. There's nothing wrong with doing this. It will still work. However, when you are proving a point or showing something as being effective, true stories are best.

To summarise

People love and remember stories.

The very best way of teaching and explaining anything is by using stories.

Chapter 21: Preparing Your Tv/Radio Interview

1- Making it interesting

Any subject can be interesting to some people, and boring or simply uninteresting to others. You have to keep in mind that whatever the subject is, there is someone out there interested in it. And no matter how uninteresting you might find it at first sight, you can make it interesting. It's your mission, as a journalist and public speaker, to dig deeper into your subject, and turn it into something interesting for most viewers and listeners out there.

Any topic, if well-presented and properly explored, can get most of the audience interested. You just have to get interested yourself, and explore the most promising aspects of the subject, aspects that make the subject more familiar and relatable to the largest number of viewers and listeners, aspects that make the subject a potential common experience that might enrich anyone's life.

In order to be able to achieve that, and make most of the audience interested, you have to relate yourself to the subject, embrace it, adopt it. It's your own project now. Get yourself extremely committed to sharing it. Keep in mind that even the most ordinary events and facts of life have some people's lives evolving around it. This is how, ultimately, it turns out there isn't a single subject that can't be made interesting.

-Own The Spotlights

2- Defining your job

When it comes to TV/radio interviews, TV/radio presenters sometimes makes the common mistake, during an interview, of telling the story themselves. When, in fact, it's certainly not your job as in interviewer to tell the story. Your job is to bring it out of your guest in the most appropriate and elegant and convincing way for the benefit of the audience. And you should help your guest do that. He's not always an expert on TV/ radio shows; you're supposed to be that expert. And with enough practice and persistence, you will be.

On the other hand, guests sometimes make the common mistake of thinking that they are the story themselves. This is the case only if your guest is a public figure, in which case there will be a thin line between him and his story, achievements, and latest news. Only then, it's all right to make the interview about him as well as his latest works. Otherwise, it's always about the topic of the interview, and not about the guest elaborating this topic.

For example, while interviewing a representative and member of a non-governmental organisation (NGO), the subject is the NGO's latest achievements, not the guest's achievements as a member of that NGO. If your guest is a cook, the interview subject that might interest the audience is his recipes, not his triumph making dinner for 500 guests last weekend. Welcoming a doctor on the show is intended to enlighten the audience about common diseases and prevention methods. You can't

let your guest doctor use precious airtime to talk about a successful routine operation he did yesterday, even though he might try to benefit from this exposure to talk about his success. Your job in that case is to remind your guest of the main subject, and put him back on track. Remind them and yourself that neither you nor they in person are the subject of audience interest. Audiences are interested in 'the story'. The guest's responsibility is to tell the story. Your job as TV/radio presenter is to get it out of him in the most amazingly interesting context, no matter how ordinary it might sometimes sound to you at first. Remember what we mentioned before: Get yourself interested in the subject, so you can present it in an interesting way, and get most of the audience to enjoy it.

3- Researching your subject

It's like the homework, the preparation for the final exam: the better you prepare yourself, the better your grades will be. And the more you research the interview subject, the more you are setting yourself up for a successful interview.

On one hand, the more you research your subject, the more questions you'll have about it, and your question list will get richer and much more interesting with every question you add.

On the other hand, the more you research your subject, the more you shield yourself from any unexpected response or turn of events during the interview. We've seen it happen repeatedly: guests storming out in the middle of an interview, others getting offensively aggressive, and some answering something the TV/radio presenter didn't even ask about. All because they have a hidden agenda that they threw in the presenter's face, on air, in the middle of the show. In other words, you should always be ahead of the game, that you're well prepared for any unexpected turn of events. Research is your weapon against such undesirable interview disasters.

I'm not trying to scare you. Quite the opposite; I'm preparing you to be unfazed in the face of any unexpected situation. I'm preparing you to be in control, so that you can be relaxed throughout all kinds of topics and any unfortunate events that you might encounter.

4- Asking the questions

You have to be well informed about the subject of the interview. You have to be well prepared. Just keep in mind, that during an interview, it's not your story that should be told, and it's not your job to tell the guest's story. Your job specifically is to get your guest to tell his story. And if you're well informed about the subject, you're expected to bring the subject out of your guest, and give him the chance to tell his story in the most successful way.

Accordingly, the question form should be formulated in such a way that it asks about the subject matter and leaves all the interesting details for the guest to tell himself.

Preparing Your TV/Radio Interview-

5- Preparing your interview plan

Do not confuse doing research with being prepared. Those are two independent tasks that work in parallel to complete each other.

While research will back you up with all the required information about the subject, up to that point all that information is still sitting on paper, in a rather disorganised manner, and some of it is still in your head. But none of that information is set in the form of a question and according to a logical conversation plan. Doing relevant research, without preparing your question list and plan, is like doing half your homework. And up to that point you can easily start your interview, then suddenly go mute and have no idea what to ask next, or how to lead the conversation further. That is, unless you back yourself up with a clear list of questions, set in a detailed yet concise interview plan, you will not do an effective job of interviewing your guest. And we will explore how to prepare "the interview plan", in details, in the following Chapter 6.

Chapter 22: Elevating Daily Conversation

You're really good at being the way you are. We all are, because we tend to do things the same way, every day, out of **habit.**

We have ingrained routines for the way we brush our teeth, make the coffee, travel to work, and greet our friends and colleagues. We no longer have to think about how to do these things because we've become **unconsciously competent** at doing so.

Wouldn't it be great to be **unconsciously competent** at speaking and performing? To be able to riff off the cuff, worry-free, full of confidence? While by now you have likely tapped away many of the blocks that have confined you in the past, this ideal level of **ultraease**

 comes from repetition – practice increases confidence – plus some positive memories of success. Speaking our truth doesn't have to be limited to the domain of public speaking. In fact, both the development and delivery of your presentations will be naturally enhanced as you become more and more comfortable and confident with every conversation. And what is public speaking if not an artful conversation with your audience?

Challenge yourself to change one small thing about the way you communicate with others every day. Here are some suggestions:

On the telephone

- Initiate a conversation rather than waiting for the other person to call you
- Choose a different greeting than normal when you answer the phone
- Before picking up, take a full breath and make a conscious decision to really hear the person on the other end – channel your inner psychic and read between the lines
- Ask more questions than you normally do, seek to better understand what the

other person is saying before you respond with your point of view
Invite the other person to really listen to you; ask "Guess what happened to me today?" or solicit their advice with "I want to tell you about a challenge I'm having and then get your advice"

Shopping

Engage the salesperson for help or an opinion (even if you don't really need it); practice looking them in the eye, ask a clarifying question, offer thanks

At work

Choose to speak with someone that you normally avoid; if they intimidate you, strike up a conversation, or say a kind word to someone who normally irritates you. You'll be amazed at how the shift in **your**
energy and intention alters your experience of being with the other person. In meetings, do something different. If you typically remain silent, allow yourself to ask a question. If you often tune out during meetings in order to frantically plan in your head what you'll say next, practice

listening fully to others speak while trusting that the connections between your heart and mind will deliver you with an appropriate, thoughtful response.

At Home

Pick an every day dialogue and mix it up.

- Your partner asks what you want for dinner and you usually say "I don't care – whatever you want is fine". Try offering an opinion instead. Or just choose something that sounds yummy and make a solid request: "I love that meatloaf you cook – can we have that tonight, please?"
- Ask for someone's opinion about the outfit you've chosen to wear – how could it be better, you wonder outloud? Find a way to compliment **their** style.
- Share something unusual at the breakfast or dinner table – tell a joke, relay a childhood memory, ask everyone to share their most recent weird dream and offer an interpretation.

Chapter 23: How To Prepare To Give The Speech Of Your Life

Like any activity, when it comes to public speaking, practice makes perfect. Even the best of the best practice and practice and practice. Martin Luther King agonized for weeks and weeks over getting his "I Have a Dream" speech just perfect. Steve Jobs used to spend days and days and days repeatedly rehearsing his product presentations. Behind every great speech, there's a lot of preparation.

Read on to discover some simple steps for creating, refining, and perfecting your speech and it's delivery...

Steps to Preparing the Perfect Speech

Here are five steps to preparing a great speech...

Determine the purpose (and topic) of your speech. Before you do anything else, you must know exactly what you hope to accomplish with this speech. Once you've determined the end you hope to achieve (the purpose of the speech), you need to decide on a topic and core message. For example, if your talk is on global warming, will your core message be to plant more trees? To invest in clean energy? To reduce your emissions? As you can see, the same topic can have many different core messages. Determine what your core message will be so you can frame the rest of your presentation around that.

Outline your speech. If your speech doesn't have structure, your audience will get lost and your "speech" will be little more than a randomly assembled collection of incomplete thoughts. Once you've identified a topic and purpose (or core message) for your speech, start outlining your main supporting points. You can also start outlining your introduction (such as what attention grabber you might kick off speech with), supporting evidence, stories, examples, engaging points, and so on.

Write your speech. Now that you've determined the purpose of your speech and done a rough outline, it's time to start your first draft. Once you've fleshed out your outline into a rough draft, you'll want to interactively edit and refine your speech, moulding it into its most effective form. That said, if you're just giving a short, informal speech, you could stop at the outline level and wing it from there. However, if you're giving a more important or formal speech, or if the stakes are higher (or if you're getting paid to speak), you will almost certainly want to flesh it out in more detail, write it up, and practice, practice, practice so you can get used to the flow of your speech and memorize it.

Add gestures, tonality, and visuals. Public speaking is not public reading. You don't just print out your draft and read it off a piece of paper. Unfortunately, many people act as if they just need to read their speech from memory. But a speech is so much more. You need gestures. You need verbal expression. And in many cases, you'll need visuals. A speech isn't something to be read—it's not a book or an essay—a book is something to be listened and watched, like film or theatre. So practice your speech in front of a mirror or video camera and add gestures as well as vocal inflections and expressiveness. Keep in mind that gestures and vocal expression should come naturally—you don't want them to look and sound artificial or forced. Moreover, planning out gestures and tonality will confuse you and distract you from what you need to say. Instead, the best route is to practice your speech until gesturing and vocal expressiveness becomes natural.

Practice and seek feedback. Get a friend, spouse, one of your children, or anybody else and practice giving them your speech or presentation. Not only can they give you feedback, but simply practicing in front of somebody else will make you more aware of any wording or expressions that sound silly, awkward, or a bit odd. It will also help you to be a little bit less nervous. Even practicing in front of someone you know and love (such as a friend or family member) can make you a little nervous, which will help to prepare you a bit for speaking to a larger audience.

Now let's take a look at a simple guideline for creating a great presentation...

The 10/20/30 Formula for the Perfect Presentation

If your speech is going to be accompanied by a PowerPoint presentation, you'll want to read this section...

Far too many people make the mistake of having countless slides, filling those slides from top to bottom with walls of text in small font, and rambling on for a tediously long time.

Fortunately, there's a simple formula that can help you avoid all of these mistakes. Brainchild of the venture capitalist Guy Kawasaki (https://guykawasaki.com/), it's called "The 10/20/30 Rule of PowerPoint."

(Note: Once again, consider how this applies to your specific circumstances or purpose. This rule doesn't necessarily need to be followed to the letter. It is also worth noting that Kawasaki intended his "10/20/30 Rule" to be used by entrepreneurs pitching their startup to venture capitalists—not as a universal presentation template. That said, it undoubtedly serves as a great template for creating a great presentation.)

Here's how the 10/20/30 rule works:

Ten slides. Your audience won't be able to comprehend or remember more than ten concepts. Don't bombard them with several dozen slides. Keep it simple. Another advantage to this is that it means your audience will be fully focused on you and what you're saying rather than taking in a new slide every ten seconds.

Twenty minutes. Guy Kawasaki recommends entrepreneurs give their ten slides in twenty minutes, allowing the remaining 40 minutes (assuming it's an hour-long meeting) for people arriving late, leaving early, technical problems (such as the projector playing up) as well as answering questions and having a discussion. Consider how this compares to your situation and the purpose of your speech and adjust accordingly.

Thirty-point font. Don't make the mistake of having tiny font that nobody can read. You want your audience to be able to read what you've got on your slide. More than that, you don't want your slide filled with a wall of text in a tiny font. You want your audience to be listening to you, not reading off your slide.

Something else you'll also want to consider is the importance of visuals. Rather than just filling your PowerPoint slides with text, use visuals (such as a relevant image, illustration, diagram, graph, etc.) to help your audience comprehend your points.

Moving on, let's now take a look at some of the best ways to quickly and efficiently memorize your speech...

How to Quickly and Efficiently Memorize Your Speech from Start to Finish

Almost everybody is, on some level or another, petrified of public speaking. And much of this fear of public speaking stems from the fear that we will forget what we need to say and just freeze up in front of everybody.

Fortunately, there are ways you can help ensure you don't draw a blank and forget your speech in front of your audience.

When you're able to recall your speech from memory, you'll not only be noticeably more confident, but you'll also be able to maintain eye contact and overall be a more powerful and dynamic speaker. Your audience will also perceive you to be more knowledgeable and credible as well.

Read on for a few different ways of memorizing your speech...

Speech Memorization Technique #1: How to Memorize Your Speech Word for Word

The first step to memorizing your speech verbatim is to write out your speech in full. Then print it out and walk around your home (so you stay awake and alert) and read it out loud a few times. Then read out only the first sentence. Memorize it. Read out the first sentence from memory without looking at your printed text. Then do the same for the second sentence, until you have the first two sentences fully memorized. And so on, until you have memorized the first paragraph and can read it from memory. And on, and on, until your entire speech is memorized.

Once you can give your entire speech from memory (and have practice it a few times in this manner), go do something else for several hours. Then, later that day (or the next day), come back and see if you can still give your entire speech from memory. You will have most likely forgotten several parts of it, so repeat the process.

This technique can work for short speeches, however I would not recommend you use this technique for longer speeches. If you do, you may end up forgetting parts of your speech due to the stress of actually being in front of a real audience (as opposed to practicing in the comfort of your home).

Another downside is that, if you're not careful, you can come off as aloof and a bit distant (which your audience will feel) as you recite your memorized speech. You also run the risk of the speech sounding unnatural and too forced, as if you're reading off a piece of paper rather than having an naturally flowing conversation with the audience.

Speech Memorization Technique #2: Create a Memory Palace

Us humans are terrible at memorizing verbatim text. It can be done, but it's hard and typically only any good for short speeches.

If you need to give a longer speech, or if you want your speech to flow better and sound more natural, you're going to have to use a technique that works better with how your brain works. This is a technique used not only by many professional public speakers, but also by memory champions.

Instead of trying to remember verbatim text, you remember things that the brain has evolved to naturally be better at remembering: images, concepts, stories, and the relationships between ideas.

For example, if I asked you to remember a random phone number or remember that the granny across the road who used to bake delicious jam scones got run over by a purple Ferrari last weekend while at church... well, I think you get the idea. You're obviously going to have a much easier time remembering what happened to the granny. Your brain is just much better at remembering images and stories than it is at remembering isolated pieces of information.

You can use this to your advantage with the memory palace technique. Here's how it works:

Create an in-depth outline for your speech. Your attention grabber, your main points, any examples, stories, or evidence you'll need, and so on.

Attach certain images to each part of your outline. Make sure they are memorable images, such as a fluffy pink elephant sitting outside your home, or a big sumo wrestler bouncing on your bed, or a jug of frozen blood in your freezer. Also make sure that they are somehow related to each part of your outline, reminding you of what to speak about. You can also organize everything (in your mind) so that as you walk through your home (in your mind), your speech is in the right order.

To give your speech, mentally walk through your home. As you walk through your home, you'll see all of these bizarre things you've placed there, which will remind you of exactly what you need to talk about in each section of your speech. As you finish each section or paragraph of your speech, walk into the next room. And so on, until you've given your entire speech.

Conclusion

These ten tips for reducing stress before doing a speech have been a great help to me who has always been paralyzed because of stress. I believe that it is for everyone to be able to speak freely and confidently, but like everything in life, if you want to succeed in it, it requires hard work. Take good note of the above, get some practice, and you will see the difference very soon. Remember that all great speakers from all time were always the ones struggling with stress and anxiety. It only is when you know your fear that you can overcome it.

www.ingramcontent.com/pod-product-compliance
Lightning Source LLC
Chambersburg PA
CBHW072007070526
44583CB00015B/1372